CHRONICLE OF A PHARAOH

THE INTIMATE LIFE OF AMENHOTEP III

CHRONICLE OF A PHARAOH

THE INTIMATE LIFE OF AMENHOTEP III

JOANN FLETCHER

Foreword by George Hart

OXFORD
UNIVERSITY PRESS

Chronicle of a Pharaoh

First published in the United States of America in 2000 by
Oxford University Press, Inc.
198 Madison Avenue, New York, N.Y. 10016–4314
Oxford is a registered trademark of Oxford University Press

Conceived, created, and designed by
Duncan Baird Publishers, London, England

Library of Congress Cataloging-in-Publication Data

Fletcher, J. (Joann)
    Chronicle of a pharaoh : the life of Amenhotep III / by Joann Fletcher.
    p. cm.
    Includes bibliographical references and index.
    ISBN 0-19-521660-1
    1. Amenhotep III, King of Egypt. 2. Pharaohs--Biography. I. Title.

DT87.38+
932'.014'092--dc21
[BB]
                                                    00-027697

Consultant: Peter Bently
Senior editor: Joanne Levêque
Editor: Charles Philips
Senior designer: Steve Painter
Designer: Rachel Goldsmith
Picture researcher: Julia Ruxton
Commissioned artwork: Louisa St. Pierre, Tony Townsend
and Fred van Deelen
Decorative borders: Louisa St. Pierre, Fred van Deelen and Egyptian Culture
Centre, Waseda University
Maps: Charlotte Wess
Reconstructions: Stephen Conlin

Typeset in Apollo, Caslon 3, Caslon 540 and Glyph Basic
Color reproduction by Colourscan, Singapore
Printed in Hong Kong by Imago

NOTE
The abbreviations CE and BCE are used throughout this book:
CE Common Era (the equivalent of AD)
BCE Before the Common Era (the equivalent of BC)

FRONTISPIECE:
The two giant statues of Amenhotep III known as the "Colossi of Memnon"
(see page 142).
TITLE PAGE:
The smiling face of a brown-quartzite head of Amenhotep III.

10 9 8 7 6 5 4 3 2 1

Contents

FOREWORD

In Luxor Museum there is a royal red quartzite statue (illustrated left), which for its serene beauty is unrivaled among the thousands of sculptures surviving from ancient Egypt. The pharaoh Amenhotep III takes the pose of a god-king, wearing a crown that symbolizes his authority over the Nile Valley and the Delta as well as identifying him with the creator god Ra-Atum (see pages 124–125). The iconographic claims of this superb statue are fully consistent with Amenhotep's supremacy as a ruler, presiding over a civilization at its zenith almost 3,500 years ago, and embodying the sun god in opulent earthly form.

Dr. Joann Fletcher's intense interest in Amenhotep III is long standing, sustained through her heavy schedule of Egyptological and archaeological research. She has avidly absorbed the recent in-depth studies into every aspect of Amenhotep's rule by scholars such as Arielle Kozloff and Betsy Bryan, and in this book she has presented all the historical, archaeological, and artistic findings in a comprehensible way.

Is Dr. Fletcher's unashamed promotion of this pharaoh justified in historical terms? One has only to undertake a brief survey of Amenhotep III's legacy to be convinced that her passion is understandable. No reign has produced such outstanding sculpture in either human or animal form. Then there is the correspondence between Amenhotep III and his colleague rulers in the ancient world, miraculously preserved in the Amarna Letters—a gem of an insight into diplomacy in the Middle East in the 14th century BCE. And what a mine of information we have regarding the pharaoh himself in the "news bulletins" carved on his commemorative scarabs: his marriage to Queen Tiy, the great lake that he dug for her, his diplomatic marriage to a foreign princess, his prowess in hunting lions and bulls.

It is poignant to consider that his monuments have been ravaged by natural processes, human antagonism, or indifference to the past. His funerary temple at Kom el-Hetan in Western Thebes, in its day the most architecturally lavish monument to a pharaoh's memory ever conceived, survives only in two colossal quartzite statues abused with the graffiti of Graeco-Roman tourists. Nevertheless, confidence oozes from every extant hieroglyph and relief carved in his reign—and, unlike some of his successors' inscriptions, the claims of Amenhotep III truly reflect the apogee of Egyptian influence.

I take great pleasure in recommending this book to anyone eager to be informed about the pharaoh Amenhotep III. Joann Fletcher's well-argued narrative brings to life those prosperous and almost hedonistic years when Egypt was under the rule of the "Dazzling Sun" himself.

George Hart, British Museum

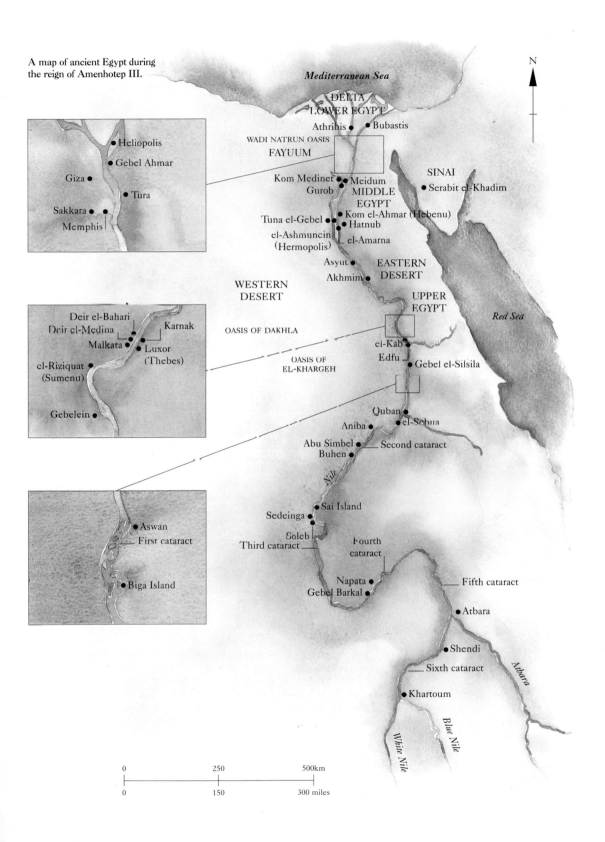

A map of ancient Egypt during the reign of Amenhotep III.

Chapter One

HE WHO DESIRES STRENGTH

ca. 1403–1392 BCE

The rejuvenated face of Amenhotep III—his wig set
with the protective uraeus serpent—is shown in
this detail from his tomb in the West Valley, Thebes.

THE BIRTH OF A GOD

A little over 3,400 years ago, in a royal palace by the Nile, a young woman gave birth to her first son—the future Amenhotep III. The woman was Mutemwia, one of the wives of the teenage prince Tuthmosis, who in turn was one of the sons of the reigning king, Amenhotep II, by Tiaa, his second queen. Tiaa was a high-ranking priestess of the state-god Amun at Karnak temple and she appears to have doted on her son Tuthmosis. In the first years of his reign Amenhotep II had crushed a rebellion in Palestine, making a show of strength that his son Tuthmosis IV was to imitate at the start of his own reign.

This *was* scepter (scepter of power) in blue faience is almost 7ft (2m) tall and bears the names and titles of Amenhotep II. It was found in a chamber in the temple of Seth at Nubt ("Tukh").

Mutemwia's son was named Amenhotep—"Amun is content"—after his illustrious grandfather, the reigning king. The baby was also given the additional name *mer-khepesh*, or "he who desires strength"; his elder name-sake Amenhotep II had proved a strong and often ruthless monarch, who upheld Egypt's policy of aggression beyond the country's northeastern borders. Having liberated Egypt from a century of foreign occupation by the *hyksos* (literally "rulers of foreign lands"), Amenhotep II's predecessors had consolidated the area of Syria-Palestine and stationed garrisons among the vassal states left in place.

Following Amenhotep II's accession some of the Syrian states rebelled against their new overlord. The young king's response was immediate: after a crushing campaign Amenhotep II executed seven of the rebel leaders in time-honored fashion by smashing in their skulls. Their corpses were hung upside down from the prow of his ship: he made a triumphant return to Memphis, where he was greeted by his wife, Queen Tiaa, then traveled on south to present the battle spoils to the state-god Amun at Karnak. There, six of the corpses were hung from the city walls of Thebes, while a seventh was taken further south still and suspended from the walls of the city of Napata, "in order to cause to be seen the victorious might of his majesty for ever and ever." Such swift retribution was clearly effective, for the vassal states remained generally loyal for the rest of the reign, each trying to outdo the others in the gifts they sent to Egypt. But their fawning made little impression on this forthright king, who never hid his contempt for his former enemies, especially when he had been drinking.

Amenhotep II was a vigorous, athletic figure, who, because of his skilled horsemanship, had been put in charge of his father's stables while he was still a young prince. He enjoyed rowing and hunting and his prowess in archery was legendary: a stela found at Giza, in the area where he trained his horses, states that the pharaoh could shoot arrows from his chariot straight through copper targets 3 inches (7.5 centimeters) thick, using a bow no one else had the strength to use.

As the birth of Amenhotep II's grandson approached, Mutemwia would have been placed in the care of the royal midwife, and watched over by the dwarf god Bes, protector of all women in childbirth, and the goddess Hathor. The experience of giving birth in ancient times was hazardous and mothers-to-be were believed to need magical protection from the gods. In Egypt, Hathor was invoked during labor with a spell for hastening birth that asked her to appear "bringing the sweet north wind." In one earlier Egyptian story referring to childbirth, it was foretold that a woman named Ruddedet would give birth to triplets who would be future kings (the first three kings of the Fifth Dynasty), so the sun god Ra sent assistance in the form of the goddesses Isis, Nephthys, Heket, and Meskhenet. They visited the woman disguised as dancers and carrying the insignia of Hathor priestesses. The woman's husband told them, "My ladies, look, the woman is in pain, her labor is difficult," to which they replied, "Let us see her, for we understand childbirth."

Mutemwia was named after the mother goddess Mut, her husband Tuthmosis's favorite deity. A black granite barque-shaped sculpture found at the Karnak temple spells out Mutemwia's name in a rebus: Mut-em-wia, meaning "Mut is

The mother goddess Mut—after whom Amenhotep III's mother was named—wears the vulture head-dress and double crown of Upper and Lower Egypt. This head is from a monumental limestone figure from Karnak temple.

in her barque." The piece was made during her son's reign and its inscriptions reflect her later elevated position: "great royal wife, the god's mother Mutemwia, great of praise, well disposed, sweet of love, who fills the hall with the fragrance of her dew, mistress of Upper and Lower Egypt, the god's mother who bore the king, praised one of the good god, for whom everything that she commands is done. May she occupy her seat within her barque, it being made as an eternal construction, for the king's mother Mutemwia."

THE DIVINE CONCEPTION OF PRINCE AMENHOTEP

Prince Tuthmosis acknowledged the future Amenhotep III as the "son of his body," but during his own reign Amenhotep introduced the legend of his divine conception. Scenes from the Birth Chamber of the Luxor temple to Amun (see pages 114–117) are accompanied by inscriptions that hail Mutemwia as "great of grace, mistress of the Two Lands, the king's mother," and name his father as none other than Amun-Ra, king of the gods. In an inscription from western Thebes, Amun hails Amenhotep III as "my son of my body, my beloved Nebmaatra, my living image, my body's creation, born to me."

At Luxor we can follow the great king from his divine conception right through his life, and beyond. The story begins with Amun diplomatically taking the form of Tuthmosis to visit Mutemwia, who is asleep in the inner rooms of her palace. According to the inscriptions that accompany the temple reliefs, "She awoke on account of the aroma of the god and cried out before him ... He went to her

straight away, she rejoiced at the sight of his beauty, and love for him coursed through her body. The palace was flooded with the god's aroma.

"Words spoken by Mutemwia before the majesty of this great god Amun-Ra: 'How strong is your power! Your dew fills my body,' and then the majesty of this god did all that he desired with her. Words spoken by Amun-Ra: 'Amenhotep, ruler of Thebes, is the name of this child I have placed in your body ... He shall exercise the beneficent

kingship in this whole land, he shall rule the Two Lands like Ra forever.'" The sandstone reliefs depict the couple's fingers touching briefly—and in this auspicious instant Amenhotep, son of Amun, is conceived.

Further images show the clearly pregnant Mutemwia being led by the hand by Hathor, goddess of love, and the ram-headed creator god Khnum fashioning the child and its *ka* (soul) on his potter's wheel as Amenhotep III is born in the presence of the gods.

A detail of reliefs in the "birth room" at the Luxor temple shows the blessed moment in which the future Amenhotep III, the chosen one of Amun, was conceived.

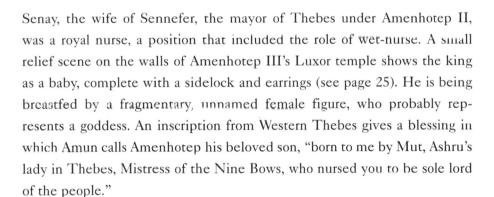

THE SPHINX'S PROMISE

YEAR 25 OF AMENHOTEP II (ca. 1402BCE)

As Amenhotep II's reign drew to its peaceful close, ancient Egypt was entering the greatest era of prosperity it would ever know. An army of royal officials efficiently administered the country on the king's behalf and was rewarded with statuary and beautifully decorated tombs in the Theban necropolis. The future Amenhotep III, still an infant, was entrusted to the care of faithful nurses while his father, Prince Tuthmosis, learnt the art of state-craft and pursued his favorite pastimes of hunting and chariotry in the desert. It was there that Tuthmosis was to have his Sphinx dream, in which he was promised the throne of Egypt.

Senay, the wife of Sennefer, the mayor of Thebes under Amenhotep II, was a royal nurse, a position that included the role of wet-nurse. A small relief scene on the walls of Amenhotep III's Luxor temple shows the king as a baby, complete with a sidelock and earrings (see page 25). He is being breastfed by a fragmentary, unnamed female figure, who probably represents a goddess. An inscription from Western Thebes gives a blessing in which Amun calls Amenhotep his beloved son, "born to me by Mut, Ashru's lady in Thebes, Mistress of the Nine Bows, who nursed you to be sole lord of the people."

Senay and Sennefer are depicted on the walls of the wonderful tomb that was given to Sennefer by Amenhotep II. The ceiling of the tomb is decorated with painted representations of grapes and Sennefer's figure appears all around the walls in the company of his family and the gods. Sennefer's granite statue was set up at Karnak and is unusual in being one of the very few pieces signed by its creators, the sculptors Amenmes and Djedkhonsu. It gives an idea of the appearance of two of the pharaoh's high officials at this time: the mayor is depicted as a wealthy man adorned

This fragmentary tomb-stela relief is from the Sakkara tomb of Meryra, an "overseer of nurses."

with golden *shebyu* necklaces as a mark of honor. The rolls of fat around Sennefer's torso are intended to indicate his élite and largely sedentary lifestyle. His wife, who is at his side, is shown in formal dress, wearing a huge tripartite wig.

Royal nurses played an important and prestigious role at court and were often honored by the pharaohs they served. Amenhotep II, the baby Amenhotep's grandfather, had been breastfed by the lady Amenemopet, whose own son Kenamun was brought up with the young prince and was to be his lifelong friend. A later scene from the Royal Tomb at Amarna depicts a nurse, shaded by a fan-bearing attendant, holding a royal baby in her arms; it has been suggested that the child is the infant prince Tutankhaten (later Tutankhamun). The tomb of Tutankhaten's wet-nurse, Maya, has recently been discovered at Sakkara.

The title "nurse" was not reserved for women. Men could also be nurses —the title covered their roles as guardians and tutors. Heqarneheh was "nurse of the king's son Amenhotep III" and at least five royal princes originally appeared in his tomb scenes. Heqarneheh's father, Heqareshu, who was "overseer of royal nurses" and a nurse to Prince Tuthmosis, is portrayed cradling four small princes on his lap in his own tomb scenes.

Another "overseer of nurses," Meryra, also administered the baby Amenhotep's estates in his additional role as "chief steward of his majesty when a child." Later promoted to the office of chancellor, the trusted Meryra was given a fine burial in Sakkara, where stela reliefs from his tomb portray him holding Prince Siatum, possibly one of Amenhotep III's brothers, on his lap (see left). Meryra's wife Baketamen sits beside him.

While his son Amenhotep was growing up, Prince Tuthmosis indulged in the traditional royal pursuits of archery, hunting, and chariotry, spending much of his time speeding around the city of Memphis in a chariot driven by "horses swifter than the wind." The teenage prince often drove out into the desert to the ancient pyramids of Giza and the sandcovered Great Sphinx, which were then already more than a thousand years old. Here, in the first years of his reign, Tuthmosis's father, Amenhotep II, had built a temple dedicated to the Sphinx as Horemakhet (a form of the sun god) and had set up a stela to honor the Old Kingdom monarchs Khafre and Khufu. Amenhotep II also created what is probably the first representation of the Aten disk (the sun disk worshiped as a god) as a human-armed sun disk. It is in this form that the Aten disk appears on a stela of Tuthmosis IV, which may have been originally carved during Amenhotep II's reign.

Amenhotep II also erected a great statue of himself between the paws of the Sphinx and it was here that Prince Tuthmosis stopped for a rest during one of his desert hunting trips. Sheltering from the midday sun in the shadow of the Sphinx's massive head, the prince fell asleep and had a dream in which the Sphinx spoke to him "as a father speaks to a son." In the dream (see pages 19–20), the Sphinx appealed to the prince to clear away the sand that had amassed around it, almost burying the front of the monument, and to restore the creature to its former glory. In exchange for this, the Sphinx promised that Tuthmosis would one day become pharaoh—the ruler of Upper and Lower Egypt.

Prince Tuthmosis dutifully cleared away the sand and undertook the restoration of the Sphinx's paws and chest. Modern excavations have revealed the mudbrick retaining walls the prince ordered to be built to protect the great monument from further sand encroachment. Although the details of the prince's accession are not known, it seems that the Sphinx fulfilled its promise: despite the fact that he had at least one elder brother, Tuthmosis did become king.

At first seemingly little more than a romantic story, the episode of Tuthmosis's Sphinx dream in fact signaled an important shift in political power and religious allegiance, since it neatly distanced the future king from the all-pervading influence of the powerful Amun clergy in Thebes, who had previously been influential in validating the heir to the throne. In the years to come, this increased identification of the pharaoh with the sun god would also culminate in the cult of the Aten sun disk (see pages 60–61) and ultimately in Amenhotep III's identification with the sun god himself (see pages 154–155).

WHAT THE ATEN ENCIRCLES

In the twenty-sixth year of his reign, when he was in his mid-forties, the warrior pharaoh Amenhotep II died. According to an Egyptian belief that was already at least five hundred years old, the king's soul was said to have risen to merge with the Aten (the sun disk worshiped as a god). During his reign the king had taken an interest in the northern-based sun cult. He had paid particular attention to the ancient site of Giza and its mighty Sphinx, constructed in ca. 2450BCE. Both Amenhotep II and his son Prince Tuthmosis (father of the future Amenhotep III) had venerated the Sphinx as the mighty sun god Ra combined with Horakhty (or "Horus in the horizon").

The mummy of Amenhotep II was found in his sarcophagus in his tomb in 1898. The king was middle-aged when he died; his mummy has wavy brown hair that has started to turn gray.

While his soul dwelt with the sun in the heavens, Amenhotep II's body underwent the traditional 70-day mummification process. Once all the vital funeral proceedings had been completed (see pages 32–33), his mummy was interred in its rock-cut tomb in the Valley of the Kings. Work on Amenhotep II's tomb—which remains one of the most impressive ancient Egyptian royal tombs—began at the start of the king's reign, giving the tomb-builders ample time in which to create a fittingly grand sepulcher, constructed to a new, regular plan. When it was discovered by Victor Loret and his team in 1898, the tomb still contained large fragments of its original funerary equipment. The excavators found themselves knee-deep in debris left behind by ancient looters: linen, furniture, funeral couches, figures of the gods carved in wood and stone, a wooden Osiris bed, amulets, and canopic jar fragments.

Much to the astonishment of the modern archaeologists, a group of reburied royal mummies was also discovered in two side chambers. It appears that the tomb had been reused by the priests responsible for restoring and reburying these mummies, including that of Amenhotep II, which was rewrapped and placed back inside its quartzite sarcophagus strewn with flowers.

In accordance with Egyptian custom, Amenhotep II's funeral rites were overseen by his chosen successor. It was the adolescent Tuthmosis who was named as heir and "eldest son of the king's body, beloved of him," in spite of the fact that he had at least one older brother (called Amenhotep).

After his father's burial, the young Tuthmosis was crowned as king. A coronation scene from the temple of Amada shows the gods placing the white-and-red double crown of Upper and Lower Egypt on the monarch's head. Tuthmosis's mother Tiaa became the most influential woman in the land and it is she, rather than any of his wives, who appears with her son in official portraiture.

Tuthmosis's birth name (his Son of Ra name) means "born of Thoth," and, on his accession, he was given four more names to make up the traditional five-part titulary of monarchy. His Strong Bull name means "perfect of diadems"; his Two Ladies name means "enduring of kingship like Atum"; his Golden Horus name "powerful of the scimitar who subdues the Nine Bows"; while, as "king of Upper and Lower Egypt," he took the throne name "Menkheperure," meaning "everlasting are the manifestations of Ra." This choice of names was intended to indicate Tuthmosis's allegiance to the sun god, a faith demonstrated by the growing status of the Aten sun disk. This is clear from another contemporary text, in which the new king is acclaimed by the gods as one "whom Amun himself magnified to be lord of what the Aten encircles, lord of the Two Lands, Menkheperure." With his father now crowned as king, the life of the infant prince Amenhotep was also about to change.

This lifesize black-granite dyad (paired statue), found at Karnak temple, represents Tuthmosis IV and his mother Tiaa, who is shown wearing the traditional vulture crown over a carefully styled wig and holding a protective arm around her son.

THE PRINCE IN THE OASIS

YEAR 1 OF TUTHMOSIS IV (ca. 1400BCE)

The newly crowned King Tuthmosis IV set up court at the traditional capital of Memphis at the apex of the Nile Delta. The royal palace was run by an army of officials, from the "overseer of the royal household," chief steward, "overseer of the royal audience chamber," and royal butler, to the heralds, messengers, and servants. The royal women also had their own staff, including the "overseer of the queen's household" and the queen's document scribe.

As well as the residence at Memphis, there was also a royal palace in the town of Gurob, which lay southwest of el-Lahun in the Fayuum oasis, on the edge of the desert. Often referred to as a harem palace—a kind of retreat for the royal family—it was a large structure of columned rooms, with storage facilities set in an enclosure to the north. Gurob Palace would originally have been beautifully decorated and furnished: pieces of imported Aegean pottery and Syrian-inspired vessels were found at the site, together with blue-glazed Egyptian pots and fragments of numerous personal items, including eye-paint containers, razors, alabaster dishes, rings, necklaces, small scarabs, and items of linen clothing.

Amenhotep seems to have spent part of his childhood in the nursery within the peaceful confines of the family palace at Gurob. A figure dedicated to Sobek Shedty, the local crocodile god, bears the inscription Amenhotep Mer-Khepesh, "Amenhotep who desires strength."

A guardian was appointed for the young prince: Sobekhotep, who was a native of the Fayuum area and the mayor of the southern lake and the lake of Sobek, as well as being the king's treasurer. Amenhotep's sister Tiaa,

The 15-tonne granite Dream Stela of King Tuthmosis IV stands between the paws of the Great Sphinx at Giza. The text inscribed on the stela, which is 12 ft (3.7m) tall, records the exact date on which it was erected: "Year 1, month 3 of the inundation, day 19" (see page 20).

named after her redoubtable grandmother, was placed in the care of Sobekhotep's wife Meryt. Prince Amenhotep and Princess Tiaa were joined by a growing number of siblings: brothers Amenemhat, Aakheperure, and Siatum, and sisters Amenemipet, Tentamun, and Petepihu.

Tuthmosis himself was busy further north in Giza, setting up a series of stelae to the gods and overseeing the completion of a limestone shrine and great granite stela, which he set up between the paws of his beloved Sphinx Horemakhet in gratitude (see page 15). Later restored by Seti I, the stela refers to Tuthmosis as son of the sun god named variously as Ra, Horemakhet, and Atum. The relief scenes that accompany the inscription show Tuthmosis offering libations and incense to the Sphinx. It has been suggested that, following Amenhotep II, subsequent pharaohs visited the Sphinx at Giza after their coronation to confirm their position. By making offerings to this massive representative of the sun god, each monarch played the part of Horus the dutiful son as he undertook the transference of royal power from his predecessors.

With his position as king duly confirmed, Tuthmosis IV could turn his attentions to the empire, with the help of men such as the overseer of soldiers, Tjanuny. The latter's Theban tomb is decorated with ranks of lively

TUTHMOSIS IV'S SPHINX "DREAM STELA"

" ... One of these days it happened that the prince Tuthmosis came traveling at the time of midday. He rested in the shadow of this great god. Sleep and dream took possession of him at the moment the sun was at its zenith. Then he found the majesty of this noble god speaking from his own mouth like a father speaks to his son, and saying, 'Look at me, observe me, my son Tuthmosis. I am your father Horemakhet-Khepri-Ra-Atum. I shall give you the kingship of the land over the living. You shall wear its white crown and its red crown upon the throne of Geb, the heir. The land in its length and breadth will be yours, and everything that the eye of the Lord of All illuminates. Good provisions will be for you from within the Two Lands, and the great produce of every foreign country, and a lifetime great in years. For many years my face has been turned to you; my heart belongs to you, and you belong to me. Behold, I am in pain, and my body is ruined. The sand of the desert upon which I used to be presses down on me. I have been waiting to have you do what is in my heart, for I know you are my son and protector. Approach me; I am with you, I am your guide.' He completed this speech. Then this prince stared because he heard this utterance of the Lord of All. He understood the words of this god and he placed silence in his heart. Then he said, 'Come, let us travel to our temple of the city, that they may set aside offerings for this god. We shall bring to him cattle and all sorts of vegetables, and we shall give praises to those who came before ...'"

Tuthmosis IV's arm brace portrays the war god Montu encouraging Tuthmosis, who is protected by Nekhbet's sister-goddess Wadjet the cobra, to execute a captive "Asiatic." As the god hands the king a scimitar, he tells him to "vanquish the lords of all the foreign lands."

soldiers often described as Nubian mercenaries; one contingent led by two trumpeters have feathers in their hair, while other groups wear protective leather nets decorated with striped animal tails over their linen kilts.

Remembering his father's swift actions against the troublesome vassal states of Syria-Palestine, Tuthmosis began pacifying his empire by launching an attack on Gezer in Palestine and Naharin in northeastern Syria. A contemporary text states: "The chiefs of Naharin bearing their revenue see Menkheperure proceeding from his house. They hear his voice like the son of Nut, his bow being in his hand like the son of Shu's successors. When he goes into battle, Aten being before him, he destroys the mountain countries, trampling the desert countries, treading to Naharin and to Karoy to ensure that the inhabitants of foreign countries are subjects to the rule of the Aten for ever."

The enemies listed in this text, from Tuthmosis's so-called "Aten" scarab, are among the twelve featured on the scenes decorating the king's chariot, which was found in pieces in his tomb. Six of these twelve enemies—Naharin, Babylonia, Tunip, the Shasu, Kadesh, and Takhesy—are from the northeastern part of the empire and beyond. The other six are African—Kush, Karoy, Miu, Irem, Gwerses, and Tiurek. The scenes show Tuthmosis protected by the vulture goddess Nekhbet and accompanied by Montu, the hawk-headed war god, firing arrows into the bodies of his Asiatic enemies, who lie strewn in piles beneath his chariot. This image is echoed on the open-work decoration of an ivory arm brace (see above), designed to protect the arm against the bowstring.

IN HONOR
OF AMUN-RA

After honoring the sun god Ra with a limestone shrine at Giza, Tuthmosis turned his attention once more to the southern capital of Thebes. He had already begun work there in the Karnak temple complex of Egypt's state god Amun, who had by now merged with the sun god to form the supreme deity Amun-Ra. During the reign of Tuthmosis IV the country continued to be administered in a highly efficient manner under well-chosen royal officials served by large numbers of scribes. Upper and Lower Egypt were divided into traditional administrative divisions known as nomes, which were managed by provincial mayors, governors, and their officials.

Tuthmosis had constructed a decorated sandstone court at Karnak (later demolished), then erected, and partially decorated, a small alabaster barque-shrine to Amun-Ra. It bore the inscription: "the King of Upper and Lower Egypt, Menkheperure: he made as his monument for his father Amun-Ra, building for him a temple of white alabaster of Hatnub." The king also decided to raise a stone obelisk that had been commissioned by his grandfather Tuthmosis III. According to its inscription, "the very great single obelisk" had "spent 35 years lying on its side in the hands of the craftsmen on the south side of Karnak" before Tuthmosis IV discovered, transported, and erected it in Karnak temple to honor his royal forebear. In 357CE the obelisk was taken to Rome, where it still stands outside the St John Lateran Church.

In ca. 1397BCE Tuthmosis ordered Neby, the mayor of Tjaru, to open new turquoise and copper mines at Serabit el-Khadim in Sinai, an area in which rich mineral deposits had been mined since the Third Dynasty. Work on the mines continued into the following year: the inscription "Year 5 under the Majesty of this good god" was found at the nearby temple to Hathor, the Egyptian goddess of love and beauty, who was known as *nebet mefkat*, or "Lady of the Turquoise," and was a patron deity of the Sinai region.

In addition to his construction programs, Tuthmosis IV set about administering his kingdom with great efficiency. Many of the names of central royal officials have survived. The highest office in the land below the king himself was that of vizier, or prime minister, a title held successively by Hepu, Ptahhotep, and Ptahmose. The overseer of the treasury was the young Amenhotep's guardian, Sobekhotep, who was later succeeded by Merire. Nebamun, for example, was appointed overseer of the deserts west of Thebes and in Year 6 he was also made chief of police. Foreign relations were the responsibility of local vassal chiefs and princes, under the supervision of Amenhotep, viceroy of Nubia, and Nehemawy, overseer of southern countries.

The clergy remained a powerful force, particularly those who were linked with the cult of Amun. The cult's high priest and prophets were based at the temple of Amun in Karnak, along with stewards, overseers of the sacred cattle, scribes, and the chief of craftsmen. Contemporary sources also mention the high priests of the gods Ptah, Montu, Onuris, Osiris, Sobek, and Ra, as well as the steward of the king's temple at Abydos and those responsible for administering the funerary temple of Tuthmosis himself at Thebes—from its high priest, Piay, to its scribe and guard.

The temple of Hathor at Serabit el-Khadim in the Sinai was built partly under Amenhotep III. Two stelae at the site record the treasury overseer Sobekhotep's later expedition to the region to fetch turquoise in preparation for Amenhotep's third *sed* festival in year 36 of the reign.

THE EDUCATION OF A PRINCE

Prince Amenhotep's education within the royal palace at Gurob was entrusted to the royal tutor Heqarneheh, who had also been one of his nurses. The prince and his brothers and sisters were taught alongside the offspring of favored officials—"children of the royal nursery"—such as Minhotep, Ptahemhet, and Paser.

Literacy was a highly prized skill, shared by an élite numbering no more than one or two per cent of the Egyptian population. Those who could read were keen to have themselves portrayed in scribal pose, seated with legs crossed and pen in hand. The "scribe in the house of the royal children," Menkheper, taught his pupils to read and write. The young Amenhotep would have been taught to write hieratic, the "shorthand" variant of the hieroglyphic script, which students practiced by copying out sections of texts and taking dictation. The prince probably would have been familiar with the Babylonian cuneiform script, the language of diplomatic correspondence between the superpowers of the time. All the children were encouraged to

Four seated scribes, holding unrolled papyrus sheets, reed pens, and wooden ink cases, are depicted in this detail of the lime-stone reliefs in the Sakkara tomb of the 18th-Dynasty General Horemheb.

read the wide variety of texts that were stored in the royal libraries. They also learnt mathematics, performing exercises that ranged from basic addition to working out the area of triangles.

In one late New Kingdom text, students were advised: "You have to do your exercises daily. Don't be idle. You begin to read a book, you quickly make calculations. Let no sound of your mouth be heard; write with your hand, read with your mouth. Ask from those who know more than you and don't be weary—try to understand what your teacher wants, listen to his instructions. 'Here I am,' you will say every time he calls you." They were encouraged to "spend the day writing and read at night; befriend the

CHILDREN'S CLOTHING

Young Prince Amenhotep wore his hair in a braid or plait at the side of his head in the "sidelock of youth"—a style that often appears in Egyptian art and has been found on the mummies of children, including that of an unidentified prince in the tomb of Amenhotep II. In one of the reliefs at Luxor, in which the baby Amenhotep is depicted being suckled by a female figure, the royal infant wears his sidelock in a plait on the right side of his head.

Children's clothes in ancient Egypt differed little from those worn by adults. Loincloths, kilts, and tunics, usually of linen, were worn by both adults and children. Detachable sleeves, designed to be sewn into sleeveless garments when the weather became cool, formed part of the young wardrobe. Archaeologists found a fine pair of such sleeves, measuring 16 inches (41 centimeters) in length and dating to this period, in a tomb at the royal palace town of Gurob.

The young daughter of the scribe Nebamun (an official under Amenhotep III) is portrayed wearing the sidelock of youth, a wide floral collar, and a gold pendant.

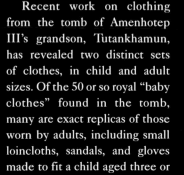

Recent work on clothing from the tomb of Amenhotep III's grandson, Tutankhamun, has revealed two distinct sets of clothes, in child and adult sizes. Of the 50 or so royal "baby clothes" found in the tomb, many are exact replicas of those worn by adults, including small loincloths, sandals, and gloves made to fit a child aged three or four years old. There is also a finely spun linen robe made for a child. It has recently been calculated that this item—which some scholars have described as the ancient equivalent of a christening robe—would alone have taken 3,000 hours (nine months of 11-hour working days) to create. Similar items to the ones belonging to Prince Tutankhamun were no doubt worn by Amenhotep III

papyrus roll and the palette—it pleases more than wine." However, sometimes a tutor would have to resort to firmer measures to keep his students' attention: "'Are you an ass? I will master you. There is no sense in your body." One proverb stated that "A boy's ear is on his back; he hears when he is beaten."

A contemporary scene in the tomb of granary official Djeserkaresonb depicts a young student carrying his papyrus roll and wooden writing board. He follows his tutor the scribe, who is shown carrying a palette containing his reed pens and blocks of black and red ink—black ink was used for writing

PALACE PLAYTIME

Toys and games were common in ancient Egypt, and royal children in particular would have had finely crafted playthings. Sophisticated manually operated toys included ivory figurines that danced and pirouetted when their strings were pulled, and animals—such as crocodiles and dogs—whose jaws opened and closed by similar means. Pull-along wheeled toys included horses, a chariot, and a model boat—complete with ramming device and steering oar—that was found at the palace site of Gurob.

Small clay models of hippopotami, crocodiles, monkeys, and other animals have also been found, their rough-hewn appearance suggesting that they were made by Egyptian children themselves.

Painting was clearly popular: a paint palette bearing a cartouche of Amenhotep III's name holds six oval blocks of colored paints, and is similar to the later ivory examples owned by his grandson, Tutankhamun, and his granddaughters, Meritaten and Meketaten. It is clear that these three royal children enjoyed unsupervised painting sessions, given the paintmarks in yellow, red, blue, and green discovered on the floor and lower sections of the walls of their playroom in the palace of Amarna, where even the original paintbrushes have been found.

Toys such as leather balls, skittles, and spining tops generated more energetic activity. Children also practiced acrobatics and dancing, and played a variety of group games such as hide-and-seek, leap-frog, and *khazza lawizza* ("jumping the goose"), which is still played in Egypt today.

Board games such as senet, hounds-and-jackals, and the snake game have also survived. Senet (meaning "to pass") was a game for two players, who would move pieces ("dancers") around by throwing a knucklebone, dice, or marked stick across a board divided into three rows of 10 squares. The board represented a journey through the underworld: four squares from the end was the "house of misfortune," and a player landing there had to start the game again; on the final squares, images of the appropriate gods were carved, ending with the falcon of the sun god Ra. The aim was to finish first, while blocking and passing your opponent. The other side of the board was often marked out to play a different game ("20 squares") and the reversible board often formed the lid of the box in which the pieces were kept.

This 18th-Dynasty wooden lion from Thebes has crystal eyes and bronze teeth. Children could make the animal's jaws snap together by pulling on a string attached to the lion's chin.

and red ink for emphasizing key words. Such equipment is identical to that found in the tomb of Tutankhamun, Amenhotep's grandson, although his writing implements are embellished with gold.

In addition to reading, writing, and mathematics, the children studied music, which played an important part at all levels of domestic life and also in temple worship. One text reminds students: "You have been taught to sing to the reed pipe, to chant to the flute, and recite to the lyre." Energetic physical activities such as running, rowing, swimming, and wrestling were also considered to be a fitting part of the palace curriculum of a student prince.

The palace pupils were taught military skills. A New Kingdom story relates how a boy was sent to school in the palace, where he "learnt to write well. He practiced all the arts of war and surpassed older companions who were at school with him." Like his father and grandfather before him, Amenhotep would have been taught how to drive a chariot and use a bow and arrow. He proved to be particularly fond of archery and hunting, pastimes that he would regularly enjoy as an adult. His grandfather, Amenhotep II, had learnt archery as a boy under the tuition of Min, mayor of This, who was full of practical advice. A scene in Min's tomb shows the mayor guiding the aim of the young prince, and is described thus: "The king's son Amenhotep taking delight in the shooting lesson in the courtyard of the palace of This. [Min] gives instruction for a lesson in shooting. He says, 'Draw your bow to your ears.'"

A fragmentary inscription from the Medamud temple of the falcon-headed war god Montu describes how such early archery practice paid off, as the ability of Amenhotep II to shoot powerfully through a copper target could not be matched by any of his officers. Amenhotep II's physical prowess is also described in detail on a stela from Giza: the inscription praises him as "a fine youth, well developed, having completed 18 years in strength," and adds that "no one could stretch his bow, nor could he be approached in running," before listing his achievements in rowing and horsemanship.

The study of mathematics formed an important part of Egyptian education. The 17th-Dynasty *Rhind Mathematical Papyrus* (a detail of which is shown here) contains equations that were used for calculating area and measuring angles.

THE HEIR APPARENT

YEARS 6–9 OF TUTHMOSIS IV
(ca. 1395–1392BCE)

King Tuthmosis's eldest son, Amenemhat, had died young and in regnal year 7 the king declared eight-year-old Prince Amenhotep to be his heir. In the same year the king promoted his sister Iaret to the position of "great royal wife." Taking Amenhotep and Iaret with him, Tuthmosis then proceeded south to crush his enemies in Nubia. Graphic scenes at Konosso, south of Aswan, depict Iaret at the king's side as he smites the Nubians before the local gods Dedwen and Ha.

This Ramesside papyrus depicts a lion (representing a king) playing a board game with a gazelle (possibly symbolizing a minor wife of the same status as Mutemwia, the mother of Prince Amenhotep).

The twin appointments of ca. 1394BCE must have greatly affected Prince Amenhotep, who was made royal heir at the same time that his aunt Iaret became his stepmother. His mother, Mutemwia, was only a minor wife and did not bear the title "great royal wife" until it was bestowed on her retrospectively by her son when he became king. Given the importance of status at court, Mutemwia—and Amenhotep—must have been only too aware of her inferior position. Even costume was designed to express an individual's relationship to the king: while Iaret and Nefertiry were, as great royal wives, entitled to wear the royal vulture and uraeus on their crowns, minor wife Mutemwia could not; instead, her crown would have been adorned with a pair of gazelle heads.

The endless potential for court intrigues increased when Tuthmosis IV added to his Egyptian wives by marrying a daughter of King Artatama I of the Mitanni, an event recalled in later diplomatic correspondence. "When

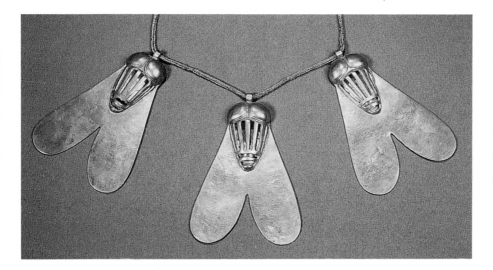

Gold "flies of valor" were awarded for courage and perseverance on the battlefield. Those pictured here were found alongside jewelry and weaponry in the early 18th-Dynasty Theban tomb of Queen Ahhotep.

Manahpiria [Tuthmosis IV] wrote to Artatama my grandfather he requested for himself the daughter of my grandfather, my father's sister, five times, six times. A seventh time to my grandfather he sent and then he gave her straight away." This diplomatic tactic—later employed by Amenhotep III—was used to seal an Egyptian-Mitannian treaty against the growing military power of the Hittites to the north, although Nubia to the south remained troublesome.

In ca. 1393BCE Tuthmosis traveled south to deal with reported trouble in the eastern desert. Sailing south from Thebes to Edfu, he then marched east down the goldmine route of the Wadi Mia to the desert mountains to tackle the Nubians, who seem to have been hindering gold shipments. Inscriptions at Konosso record the king's personal involvement in what is termed a military "skirmish": he is depicted offering wine to the gods Amun and Khnum in celebration of the campaign's successful outcome.

Further inscriptions at Konosso reveal that Tuthmosis was accompanied on his progress south by a retinue of courtiers led by the royal herald Re. Several members of the royal household also made the journey, including the princes Amenhotep and Aakheperure, who were considered old enough to travel with their tutor-guardians, father and son Heqareshu and Heqarneheh. On the outside panels of his throne Tuthmosis is shown as a rampant sphinx trampling Nubians, and hailed as "Horus with the powerful arm, effective in crushing all foreign countries." Although they were part of the empire, the threat posed by the Nubians and other peoples further south can be seen by the frequency with which they were listed among Egypt's traditional enemies.

Chapter Two

APPEARING IN TRUTH

ca. 1391–1382 BCE

This brown-quartzite head of Amenhotep III
portrays the pharaoh smiling.

THE CHILD KING

YEAR 1 OF AMENHOTEP III (ca. 1391BCE)

The so-called "Marriage Scarab," of which this is one of the 56 surviving examples, was issued in Amenhotep III's first regnal year to announce his marriage to Tiy. The scarab inscription refers to "the great royal wife Tiy, may she live, her father's name is Yuya, her mother's name is Tuya; she is the wife of a mighty king whose southern border is at Karoy and whose northern border is at Naharin."

In his tenth year of rule Tuthmosis IV died, at an age that has been estimated as anything between 25 and 40 years old. The decoration of his tomb in the Valley of the Kings was hastily completed during the 70-day mummification process and his beautifully prepared mummy was then laid to rest in its finely decorated quartzite sarcophagus. Tuthmosis's burial was accompanied by those of two of his children, his son Amenemhat and his daughter Tentamun, who had also died that year. It was the sad responsibility of the young heir, the new king Amenhotep III, to bury not only his father but also his brother and sister. Happier events, however, took place later in Amenhotep's first regnal year when, following his coronation, he married a young girl called Tiy, the daughter of provincial officials from Akhmim.

Under the caring eye of his mother Mutemwia, the 12-year-old Amenhotep led the huge state funeral for his father, brother, and sister. He participated in all the traditional funerary rites, performing the "opening of the mouth ceremony" (see page 161) as was required of the dead pharaoh's dutiful son. Tuthmosis's tomb was filled with the usual range of goods that were held to be vital for the afterlife, from canopic equipment of the king and his children to faience *shabti*s, amulets, ritual gilded figurines, model boats, vases, glassware, pottery, jewelry, mirrors, feather fans, gloves of red and green leather, finely embroidered textiles, weapons, the gilded royal chariot, and furniture, including the king's gilded throne.

Eighty years later, after a raid by tomb-robbers, the royal official Maya (whose burial was recently rediscovered at Sakkara) and his assistant

Djehutymose carefully restored the burial of Tuthmosis IV, leaving behind an inscription on the tomb wall that read: "Year 8, 3rd month of *akhet* [inundation], day 1 under the majesty of the king of Upper and Lower Egypt Djeserkheperure-setepenrc, son of Ra, Horemheb. His majesty, life, prosperity, health, commanded that the fan-bearer on the king's right-hand, king's scribe, overseer of treasury, overseer of works in the place of eternity [royal necropolis], and leader of the festival of Amun in Karnak, Maya, son of the noble Iawy, born of Lady Weret, be charged to renew the burial of King Menkheperure, true of voice, in the noble mansion upon the west of Thebes. His assistant is Djehutymose whose mother is Iniuhe of The City [Thebes]."

After yet another robbery, Tuthmosis's mummy was removed and reburied with a number of others in the tomb of his father Amenhotep II.

This detail of a painting from Tuthmosis IV's tomb depicts him with the gods of the afterlife. Left to right: the god Osiris; Tuthmosis, wearing the traditional *nemes* headcloth and kilt; Anubis; a repeated portrait of the king; and Hathor as Lady of the West. Each deity is depicted presenting the king with the gift of life (the *ankh* symbol).

The burial equipment that had been left in the original tomb was smashed and stripped of its gold. The robbers even left behind their rope, which was found still tied to one of the columns.

Following his father's burial, Amenhotep III was proclaimed pharaoh and crowned at a great state ceremony in the traditional capital Memphis. In the barque shrine of Luxor temple (see page 117) Amenhotep's coronation is depicted in relief scenes in which the king—watched by the gods—kneels to receive the crown from Amun-Ra. The god is then shown laying his hand on the solar *atef* crown to confirm that the coronation ritual has been performed correctly. Shortly after his coronation the king would have followed in the footsteps of his father and grandfather by paying homage before the Sphinx—the embodiment of the sun god—thus undertaking the transference of royal power and confirming his authority under the great creature's watchful eye.

Amenhotep III is portrayed in this head from a granite figurine—the front and back of which are shown here—wearing the double crown of a united Egypt. The white crown of Upper Egypt is shown set within the red crown of Lower Egypt; both are worn over the regal striped *nemes* headcloth.

Because of the new king's tender age, his mother Mutemwia was made his regent; the two are represented in a painted scene from the tomb of Heqareshu. Amenhotep, wearing the blue *kheperesh* crown and holding the crook, flail, and mace as symbols of his new authority, is enthroned beneath an ornate canopy, while Mutemwia stands behind him, her hand on his shoulder to indicate her guidance, and both are fanned with ostrich feathers by the royal fan-bearers.

The funerals and coronation were followed by the royal marriage of the young king and Tiy (see pages 70–73). Tiy's father, Yuya, was a priest of Min and "overseer of the cattle of Min lord of Akhmim." Her mother, Tuya, was "singer of Amun," "singer of Hathor," "chief of the entertainers of Amun," and "chief of the entertainers of Min." Amenhotep promoted his new in-laws. Yuya was made both "master of the horse" and "his majesty's lieutenant-commander of chariotry." Tuya was hailed as "king's mother of the great royal wife," and her son Anen was also elevated to high religious office, an honor in which she took great pride.

AMENHOTEP III'S NAMES AND TITLES

Amenhotep III assumed the traditional five-fold titulary of kings, taking epithets that reflected his intended policies as monarch. His birth name (the Son of Ra name) was "Amenhotep [meaning Amun is satisfied], ruler of Thebes"; his throne name, as "king of Upper and Lower Egypt," was "Nebmaatra," meaning "Ra, lord of truth"; his Horus name was "strong bull, appearing in truth"; his Two Ladies name was "he who establishes laws and pacifies the Two Lands"; and his Golden Horus name was "great of strength, smiter of the Asiatics."

Amenhotep's cartouches containing two of his royal names: "Amenhotep, ruler of Thebes" and "Nebmaatra."

I-MN-N-HTP HEKA WASET
Amenhotep, ruler of Thebes

NEBMAATRA
Ra, lord of truth

I (reed)

MN (game board)

N (water)

HTP (loaf on a reed mat)

HEKA (crook)

WASET (scepter)

NEB (lord)

RA (sun god)

MAAT (truth)

TIT-RA (image of Ra)
This symbol is an occasional addition to the basic "Nebmaatra."

AMENHOTEP'S INHERITANCE

A t his accession Amenhotep III inherited a kingdom that was already 1,600 years old, a kingdom that had been expanded into a vast empire by his Eighteenth-Dynasty predecessors. Thanks to his father's careful policies, it was also a peaceful empire—even its previous rivalry with Mitanni had been ended by Tuthmosis's diplomatic marriage to the daughter of the Mitannian king Artatama I. Amenhotep's Egypt was the most powerful nation in the ancient world and enjoyed good relations with the other major powers of Babylon, Assyria, Arzawa (western Anatolia), Alashiya (Cyprus), and Hatti (Hittites) as well as Mitanni, the rulers of all of which addressed Amenhotep as "my brother" (see pages 150–153).

Although they were never under Egyptian control, official propaganda still claimed that Pharaoh ruled supreme over Assyria and Babylon and as far as Greek city-states such as Mycenae. In reality, the extent of the Egyptian empire reached "from Karoy to Naharin"—Karoy in the Sudan was the region between the fourth and fifth cataracts (areas of rocky rapids in the mid-Nile Valley) extending out to the eastern gold mines, and Naharin was the name for Mitanni on the Upper Euphrates. Within the empire, the vassal states of Syria-Palestine were divided into three areas, each of which had its own Egyptian governor, who held the title "overseer of northern countries" (see pages 74–75). In Nubia the area ruled by an Egyptian-style administration was headed by the extremely powerful official the "Viceroy of Kush" on the king's behalf (see pages 44–47).

In a particularly beautiful text from the king's funerary temple at Kom el-Hetan, the god Amun gives the king dominion over the four corners of the world. "Speech of Amun, King of the Gods: 'My son of my body, my beloved Nebmaatra, my living image ... born to me by Mut, Ashru's lady in Thebes, mistress of the Nine Bows, who nursed you to be sole lord of people. My heart is very joyful when I see your beauty. I did a wonder for your majesty. Turning my face to the south I did a wonder for you, I made the chiefs of wretched Kush come before you, carrying their tribute on their backs. Turning my face to the north I did a wonder for you, I made the countries of the ends of Asia come to you carrying all their tribute on their backs. They offer you themselves and their children, begging you to grant them the breath of life. Turning my face to the west I did a wonder for you, I let you capture Tjehenu, they can't escape! Built is this fort and named after my majesty, enclosed by a great wall that reaches up to heaven, and settled with the princes' sons of Nubian bowmen. Turning my face to the eastern sunrise I did a wonder for you, I made the lands of Punt come here to you, with all the fragrant flowers of their lands, to beg your peace and breathe the air you give.'"

The bound and prostrate Nubian captives shown in this detail from Tutankhamun's ceremonial footstool represent four of the "Nine Bows," the nine traditional enemies of Egypt.

HIS FATHER'S SON

YEAR 2 (ca. 1390BCE)

After overseeing his father's burial, Amenhotep performed the traditional duty of a legitimate son and successor in completing Tuthmosis's building projects. He also opened new quarries to provide the materials for his own planned constructions: in the second year of his reign he opened fresh sites for limestone quarrying at Bersheh and further north at Tura, the source of some of the limestone used to build the pyramids at Giza and Sakkara more than 1,000 years earlier. The stone from such quarries was to be used in the new king's building schemes, including his additions to the temple at Karnak. Amenhotep took after his father and grandfather in his love of outdoor pursuits, particularly chariotry and big-game hunting. During Year 2 he took part in a spectacular bull hunt around the Wadi Natrun area (northwest of modern Cairo).

The bull was a symbol of royal power and its tail was worn on the king's belt as a mark of his strength and virility. "Strong bull" was a royal epithet, as was Kamutef, meaning "bull of his mother," part of a symbolism in which the king's mother took the form of a cow, the animal sacred to the goddess Hathor; Kamutef was also one of the epithets of Amun combined with Min, the god of male sexual potency. Amenhotep's Horus name was Ka-nakht kha-em-maat, "strong bull, appearing in truth."

The bull featured heavily in religious iconography: the bull of Ra was connected with solar religion, as was the Mnevis bull based at the sun god's city of Heliopolis. Similarly, the Buchis bull of Armant was regarded as the physical manifestation of Ra and Osiris, and the Apis bull of Memphis (see page 111)

Embossed figures of bound captives and delicate geometric patterns decorate this red-leather wristguard, which was found in Amenhotep III's tomb.

was seen as the embodiment of Ptah and Osiris. The priests would choose individual animals to be divine representatives on the basis of particular markings found on their hides.

Cattle were also regarded as appropriate offerings to make to the gods and in temple-relief scenes artists depicted specially fattened cattle with decorated horns. Large herds of cattle intended to be used as sacred offerings were part of the estates of the temple of Amun; a painted scene from the tomb of the scribe Nebamun shows rows of such animals being counted as their young herdsman exhorts them, "Come on! Hurry up! Don't make such a noise!"

The opening of the Tura quarries in Amenhotep III's second regnal year was accompanied by a stela inscribed: "His majesty commanded quarry chambers to be opened anew to obtain fine limestone of Ainu to build

In a fragment of a painted wall scene from the Theban tomb of Nebamun, the seated scribe (bottom register, second from the left) records the numbers of cattle herded before him.

THE WADI NATRUN HUNT

In the second year of his reign, the young Amenhotep III took part in a large-scale organized bull hunt around Wadi Natrun. Evidence of the pharaoh's passion for chariotry and hunting was found in his tomb in the form of a chariot wheel and pieces of his chariot harness, made up of red, green, and white dyed calfskin adorned with large metal studs. Amenhotep is known to have particuarly enjoyed the hunting of lions and wild bulls.

The Wadi Natrun episode is recorded on the "Wild Bull Hunt Scarab." "Regnal year 2 under the majesty of Horus: strong bull, appearing in truth; he of the Two Ladies: who establishes laws and pacifies the Two Lands;

golden Horus: great of strength, smiter of the Asiatics; king of Upper and Lower Egypt, lord of the Two Lands: Nebmaatra; son of Ra: Amenhotep, ruler of Thebes, given life; and the great royal wife Tiy, may she live like Ra. A wonder that befell his majesty. One came to his majesty saying, 'There are wild bulls upon the desert in the region of Shetep [Wadi Natrun].'

"His majesty sailed downstream in the royal barge *Kha-em-maat* ['Appearing in Truth'] during the evening, making good time, arriving in peace at the region of Shetep in the morning. His majesty appeared in his chariot with his whole army at the back of him. One instructed the officers and private soldiers in their entirety

and the children of the royal nursery to keep a watch on these wild bulls. Then his majesty commanded that a ditch be dug to surround these wild bulls, and his majesty proceeded against all these wild bulls.

"The number thereof: 170 wild bulls. The number the king took in hunting on this day: 56 wild bulls. His majesty waited four days to give rest to his horses. His majesty appeared in the chariot. The number of wild bulls he took in hunting: 40 wild bulls. Total number of wild bulls: 96."

The Wadi Natrun bull hunt seems to have been a formal, almost stage-managed event. It was intended as a very public demonstration of the king's ability to control wild forces and so bring order to chaos.

mansions of millions of years, after his majesty found the quarry chambers that were in Tura falling into great ruin since the times that were before." As the inscription states, stone was needed for Amenhotep's ambitious temple-building projects in constructing the "mansions of millions of years." At Karnak the pharaoh began the magnificent replanning and rebuilding work that would occupy him for much of his long reign. Amenhotep appears to have treated the work that earlier kings had carried out on the temple with respect, "making a temple anew without damaging what was done before."

AMENHOTEP'S KARNAK

Amenhotep's first modification at the Karnak temple was to complete Tuthmosis IV's shrine for the barque of Amun-Ra beside the fourth pylon. This was later followed by the systematic removal of his predecessors' earlier buildings in this area. Their alabaster and sandstone blocks were carefully placed deep in the foundations of Amenhotep's own third pylon (see page 54).

Amenhotep III redesigned and added to large areas of the Karnak temple complex. Together with subsidiary buildings and extensive statuary, he also erected a magnificent tenth pylon (see below), fronted by two colossal statues of the king, one of which was the largest statue ever set up in Egypt.

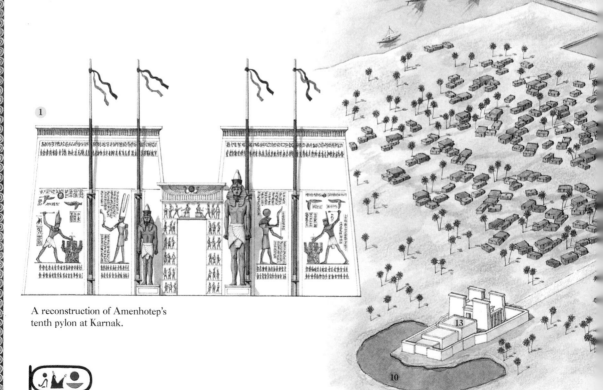

A reconstruction of Amenhotep's tenth pylon at Karnak.

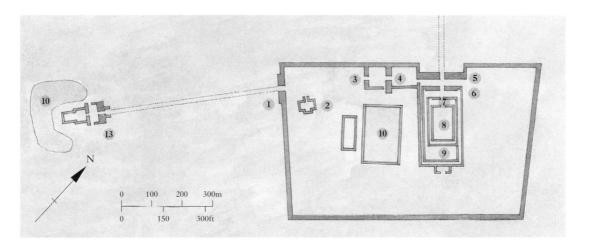

1 Tenth pylon (see reconstruction, below, left) (Amenhotep III)

2 Temple of the *sed* (jubilee) festival of Amenhotep II

3 Seventh pylon (Tuthmosis III)

4 Eighth pylon (Hatshepsut)

5 Third pylon (Amenhotep III)

6 Fourth pylon (Tuthmosis I)

7 Fifth pylon and sixth pylon (both Tuthmosis III)

8 Middle Kingdom temple buildings

9 Memorial temple of Tuthmosis III

10 Sacred lake

11 Harbor

12 Departure quay for sacred barque of Amun

13 Temple of Mut

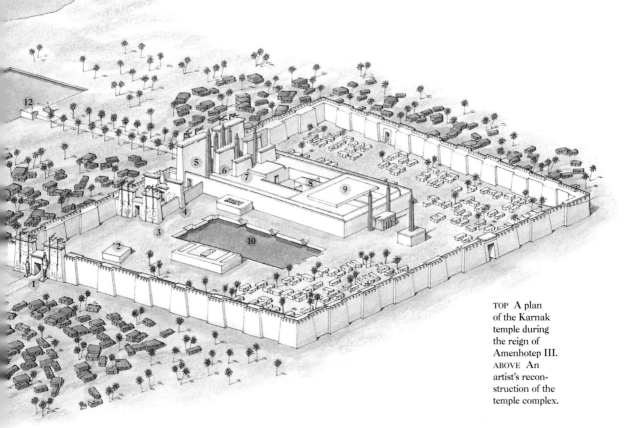

TOP A plan of the Karnak temple during the reign of Amenhotep III. ABOVE An artist's reconstruction of the temple complex.

UNDER THE VULTURE'S WING

YEARS 3–4 (ca. 1389–1388BCE)

Although he was still only 14 years old, work was already well underway on Amenhotep's tomb, as stone masons hacked into the limestone cliffs of the isolated Western Valley at Thebes. The king also continued work on the other side of the Nile, on the Theban East Bank at Karnak. At around this time a small shrine to the vulture goddess Nekhbet—one of the most important deities of the reign—was built at el-Kab at the mouth of one of the valleys leading to the Eastern Desert goldmine route. The Nekhbet shrine was among the first temples to be completed by the king.

The interior of Amenhotep's shrine to the vulture goddess Nekhbet is decorated with relief scenes depicting the king seated with his father Tuthmosis IV, both carved in the early artistic style inherited from Tuthmosis's reign. Amenhotep is shown in the company of Nekhbet, who was the mistress of Upper Egypt and a sky goddess connected with the sun gods Amen-Ra and Ra-Horakhty.

Nekhbet, with her sister-goddess and counterpart Wadjet the cobra, was responsible for the safety of the king. His Two Ladies name (one of his five royal titles; see page 35), which related directly to these two goddesses, was "Semen-hepu segereh-tawy," meaning "he who establishes laws and pacifies the Two Lands." Nekhbet's protective wings appear in ritual and secular contexts, decorating both the king's bedroom ceiling (see page 135) and the inside of his sarcophagus lid (see page 88), watching over him when he is in the most vulnerable situations—in sleep and, ultimately, in death.

In carrying out his own building projects, Amenhotep III was to change much of the Egyptian landscape. He restructured Karnak (a site known to the ancient Egyptians as Ipet-Sut, "the most favored of places"), where, as well as completing his father's barque shrine beside the fourth pylon of the temple of Amun-Ra, Amenhotep turned his attention to the temple's alignment. The king was inspired by the vision of his female predecessor Hatshepsut, who had reigned a century earlier. She had planned a north–south processional way, which Amenhotep now constructed, between Amun's temple and the Luxor temple. This restored a north–south emphasis to Karnak, replacing the east–west emphasis that had previously been imposed on the complex. Amenhotep also created new temples at Luxor on the Theban West Bank and across the length and breadth of the empire, all constructed to his new specifications.

As monumental projects began to replace small-scale constructions, Amenhotep also transformed the interior design of Egyptian temples. The cramped, closed-in style of earlier buildings was replaced by open-plan layouts with solar courts open to the sky and surrounded by tall, graceful columns, all of which typified the pharaoh's architectural tastes. His inclusion of the so-called "birth room" at Luxor is regarded as the inspiration for the birth houses (mammisi) that were included in the later Graeco-Roman temples.

During the earlier part of his reign, Amenhotep also built a limestone temple at the sun god's great cult center Heliopolis ("Iunu") in Lower Egypt. This project formed part of the king's systematic transformation of Egypt's religious policy: he envisaged a great complex of new ritual temples in which Amun of Thebes would be worshiped as the sun god Amun-Ra in appropriately magnificent surroundings. As the other deities were absorbed into the sun cult, their relevant solar epithets were emphasized and Amenhotep himself was portrayed as their representative on earth.

Amenhotep III's great royal wife Tiy is portrayed in this statuette wearing a vulture dress and head-dress and a tall double-feather crown, which associate her with the vulture goddess Nekhbet, and thus identifiy the queen as a protector of the king.

HORUS IN THE SOUTH

YEAR 5 (ca. 1387BCE)

In the fifth year of his rule Amenhotep crushed a rebellion in the far south of his empire, where the Nile meets its tributary the Atbara in northern Butana. Aged 16, Amenhotep triumphed in what proved to be the only major military encounter in his reign of almost 40 years. Egyptian troops led by Amenhotep and his viceroy Merymose defeated the rebel forces of Kush, Irem, Tiurek, and Weretj (or Weresh), taking 30,000 prisoners. His victory was commemorated on three stelae at Aswan and on Sai Island in Sudan, while a further undated and fragmentary stela at Semna may record a second minor campaign further south in Ibhet, in the desert southeast of the second cataract.

It was vital for the pharaoh to maintain firm control of his southern lands, both to keep the borders of the empire secure and to safeguard profitable trade routes. Six years after his father Tuthmosis had moved to quell a rebellion to the south, the youthful Amenhotep reacted decisively to halt a revolt in the same region. The official version, inscribed on the victory stelae, gives the following account: "Regnal Year 5, third month of the inundation, day two. Someone came to tell his majesty that 'the fallen one of vile Kush has plotted rebellion in his heart.' His majesty led on to victory, which he completed in his first campaign of victory. His majesty reached them like the wingstroke of a falcon, like Montu in his transformations ... Ikheny, the boaster in the midst of his army, did not know the lion that was before him. Nebmaatra the fierce-eyed lion, whose claws seized vile Kush, who trampled down all its chiefs in their valleys, and cast them down in their blood, one on top of the other."

This description captures the way in which Egypt's enemies are often portrayed in art. On a painted chest from Tutankhamun's tomb, the bodies of Egypt's foes pile up as they attempt to flee their fate at the hands of the

The reliefs that
decorate the
Egyptian temple
of Soleb in
Upper Nubia
(modern Sudan)
include rows of
cartouches listing
southern towns,
regions, or
groups of people
conquered by
Egypt. Every
cartouche shows
the figure of a
captive—such
as the Nubian
depicted here—
from the region
named, each with
his arms bound
behind him.

pharaoh. The allusion to the king as a lion is embodied in a tiny blue-and-gold votive head of the royal lion with the head of a Nubian enemy wedged between his golden teeth. Amenhotep's Karnak reliefs show a similar scene, with the lion-king grasping the head of an Asiatic adversary. Bound figures of Nubians and Asiatics are depicted on the soles of royal sandals and at the base of royal staffs—in both cases symbolically keeping the enemy under control and grinding them regularly into the dirt.

Unlike the vassal states in the northeastern part of the empire, which were ruled on the king's behalf by three governors, Nubia was controlled by an Egyptian-style administration led by the "Viceroy of Kush." This position was held by the trusted official Merymose throughout the reign, his territory encompassing Upper and Lower Nubia, Kush—the area south of the second cataract—and Wawat, between the first and second cataracts.

SOUTHERN RICHES

Egypt kept a close watch on its southern territories. Amenhotep called on Merymose, his dependable Viceroy of Kush, to take military action in order to preserve vital trade links, and he himself took part in what the official account called the "first campaign of victory," protecting the routes that brought the gold and minerals on which much of Egypt's great wealth was based.

In his capacity as "overseer of the gold mines of Amun," Merymose was responsible for the gold output of the Sudan area, which was divided into the "gold of Kush" obtained from the area between the second and third cataracts and the "gold of Wawat" from the Eastern Nubian desert, as well as the gold that came from the mines of Barramiya to the east of Edfu.

Unlike gold, the green mineral malachite, or copper carbonate, and the grey-black mineral galena could both be sourced in Egypt. However, the southern lands also yielded these extremely useful minerals. Reserves of malachite were found in the Eastern Desert and galena was mined in the region of Aswan. The Egyptians used malachite in smelting copper and used galena as an occasional source for lead.

The goddess Isis kneeling on the sign for "gold," from the golden coffin of Tuya, Queen Tiy's mother. Gold was valued as a mark of wealth and standing—it was used in large amounts in the burial of Tuya and her husband Yuya, indicating their royal status.

The Egyptians had recruited Nubians as mercenary troops from the beginning of the Old Kingdom. The Medjay from the eastern deserts of Nubia acted as border police and scouts, and Nubian archers in brightly colored kilts are widely represented in art. The rulers of the empire often referred to their southern neighbors as "vile" and "wretched," but it is clear that good relations existed between native Egyptians and the Nubians living in Egypt. The royal official Maiherpri, fan-bearer on the king's right hand and possibly one of the royal bodyguards, had been raised as a "child of the royal nursery" (see page 24) and was given a burial that was discovered, unplundered, in the Valley of the Kings. It is not known for certain under which king he served, but his burial equipment is consistent with the mid-Eighteenth Dynasty. His perfectly preserved mummy, with naturally dark skin and a wig made from his own tightly curled hair, clearly indicate Nubian descent, while his funerary papyri show him with black skin and the same hair type. Arrows in a leather quiver and a box of leather loincloths indicate his military occupation.

In a detail from a relief scene in the late 18th-Dynasty Sakkara tomb of the general Horemheb, Egyptian officers are shown standing guard over a group of Nubian captives while a scribe counts the number of prisoners.

OVERLEAF The sandstone temple of Soleb, where Amenhotep III was worshiped as "Nebmaatra, lord of Nubia."

PRIEST OF PRIESTS

Queen Tiy's brother Anen, portrayed in this almost life-size black-granite statue, became the powerful second prophet of Amun under Amenhotep III.

YEAR 6 (ca. 1386BCE)

At an early stage in his reign Amenhotep III started to consider moving his main residence from Memphis, the traditional royal capital, to the southern city of Thebes. He may have seen a need for the king to be located in a more central position in relation both to Egypt and to its vast empire—since the southern lands of Nubia, which stretched far down into the Sudan, equaled Egypt in extent. But other considerations may also have been guiding his thinking in this period.

Given the amount of time Amenhotep spent in Thebes and the remarkable concentration of his building work there, it would appear that he had a personal preference for the area. Thebes was celebrated as the home of the founders of both the Middle and New Kingdoms and was thus a city associated with new beginnings. Amenhotep may have wanted to move south for political and religious reasons, too, and perhaps also because he felt driven to seek an escape from the traditional atmosphere of the northern capital with its massive bureaucracy.

The young king had already shown a desire to challenge the status quo and surely realized that in doing this he would have to take on the entrenched Amun clergy, who were based at the Karnak temple in Thebes. There could have been no better place from which to keep things under control than Thebes itself. Since the beginning of the Eighteenth Dynasty the Amun priesthood had become increasingly influential and had begun to rival the king in terms of wealth and power. The Karnak priests had even become instrumental in choosing the heir to the throne, a situation that was only changed by the actions of Amenhotep's father, Tuthmosis IV, who chose to interpret his own accession as a result of the sun god's intervention.

Tuthmosis's astute act opened the way for his son to continue the process of change, which he did gradually and diplomatically. Following in the footsteps of his father and grandfather in their increasing emphasis on solar worship, Amenhotep pursued a systematic religious policy aimed at reorganizing Egypt's pantheon of deities to emphasize the gods' solar attributes. He changed the traditional way in which temples were built—from their layout to their decoration—and used nepotism in selecting religious personnel as a means of controlling events from within.

Little remains of the once-great traditional Egyptian capital Memphis. These surviving temple-column capitals are carved with the head of the goddess Hathor.

Although for practical reasons he was obliged to delegate his duties to individually appointed high priests, in theory the king himself was Egypt's high priest, the intermediary between all the gods and his people. In this role he was repeatedly depicted presenting *maat*, the symbol of truth and order, back to the gods—both to sustain them and to indicate his right and ability to rule.

In an unprecedented move, Amenhotep III gave extensive religious powers to his closest official and namesake, Amenhotep son of Hapu, not only placing the scribe's statuary throughout Amun's temple, but also granting his servant powers almost equal to his own: inscriptions on the statues state that Amenhotep son of Hapu would intercede with Amun himself on behalf of those who approached. The king's chosen man, who was not a member of Amun's clergy, could act as intermediary between the people and the gods on the king's behalf, bypassing the priesthood altogether.

Amenhotep also made his brother-in-law Anen second prophet of Amun at Karnak, a role that placed him just one step behind the high priest of Amun. A superb black-granite figure (see left) portrays Anen in priestly attire, his long linen kilt tied with a golden belt set with the king's name. His outfit is topped with a panther skin indicative of office, its pelt spangled with stars symbolizing Anen's astronomical role in the temple. As the king's close relative, Anen was the first priest in Thebes to hold the northern title "chief of sightings." This title had previously been held only by priests of Ra from the northern city of Heliopolis.

THE SERVANTS OF AMUN

Ptahmose, who is represented by this faience *shabti* figurine, held several posts under Amenhotep III, including that of high priest of Amun.

Although the role of pharaoh meant that Amenhotep III was the sole earthly intermediary between the gods and his people, for practical reasons he delegated this duty to the high priest of each deity. By the time of the Eighteenth Dynasty the most powerful deity in all Egypt was the state god Amun at Karnak, combined with the ancient sun god Ra to create Amun-Ra, king of the gods. The high priest of Amun bore the title "first prophet of Amun," and was supported in his role by the second, third, and fourth prophets.

The second prophet was responsible for the economic organization of the temple. This was an office that Amenhotep astutely gave to his brother-in-law Anen, who also held the titles "lector priest who knows the procession of the sky, chief of sightings in the great house, the *sem* priest in southern Heliopolis [Thebes], who gives offerings at the proper stations, who propitiates the gods with his voice." *Sem* priests performed the "opening of the mouth ceremony" during funeral rites and were the first priests entitled to wear the panther skin, as worn by Anen in his black-granite statue (see page 50).

Under Amenhotep, Amun's third prophet was Amenemhat, while

THE HIGH PRIEST

The high priests were the only individuals allowed to approach the gods directly within their shrines, a duty that they carried out on behalf of the pharaoh and which had to be undertaken each morning and evening. Daily offerings of fine foods, wine, incense, perfumed oil, cosmetics, and linen were presented before the cult statues, to the accompaniment of music and singing. Once he had made the offerings, the high priest would withdraw, carefully sweeping away his footprints as he went and restoring the purity of the shrine amid clouds of incense.

On the accession of Amenhotep, the position of high priest of Amun was held by Ptahmose, whose religious titles included "steward of Amun" and, because he was the chief priest of Egypt's state god, "overseer of priests of Upper and Lower Egypt." In addition Ptahmose carried out more secular tasks as "overseer of all works," mayor of Thebes and royal fan-bearer.

By year 20 Ptahmose had been succeeded as high priest by Meryptah, the "overseer of the priests of all the gods," while the title of "steward of Amun" passed to Sobeknakht.

Simut, the overseer of the treasury and "sealer of every contract in Karnak," was the fourth prophet until his promotion to the post of second prophet on the death of Anen around year 30 of the reign.

Priests were referred to as *hem netjer*, literally meaning "servant of the god," and Amun was served by a veritable army of attendants, all of whom had to be ritually pure (*waab*). They bathed four times each day in the temple lake, removing body hair and wearing pure linen robes. "Lector priests" (*hery heb*) were responsible for reading out the rituals from the sacred texts. "Hour priests"—astronomers such as Nakht—were responsible for monitoring the heavens in order to determine the correct timing of rituals and festivals.

The ritual performance of music and dance was provided by high-born women, including the king's mother-in-law Tuya, in her capacity as singer and "chief of the entertainers of Amun." The huge number of flowers used in worship were prepared by men such as another official called Nakht, "bearer of floral offerings to Amun."

In order to provide a reliable supply of flowers, grain, and sacrificial cattle, the temple of Amun owned vast agricultural estates throughout the country. These estates constituted an important force in the Egyptian economy. Heby, the mayor of Memphis and one of the many officials whose positions involved both secular and religious duties, was the "overseer of the two granaries of Amun" in the nomes (administrative districts) of Lower Egypt; his southern counterpart was a man named Amenhotep. The scribes Nebamun and Neferhotep were "counters of the grain of Amun," while the *waab* priest Pairi oversaw "the farmers of Amun." The god's estates also supplied the huge numbers of cattle needed for sacrificial offerings, which were prepared by the temple butchers.

Large communities of craftsmen were associated with the temple, where the workshops employed men such as Huy, "sculptor of Amun," and Amenhotep, "overseer of carpenters of Amun." Other "servants of Amun" combined military roles with their religious duties: the head of the royal archers, Wesi, was also the standard-bearer of the barque *Front of the Beauty of Amun*, in which the god's statue was carried in procession; the police chief Nebamun was also a ritual standard-bearer.

ADORNMENTS FOR IPET-SUT

YEAR 7 (ca. 1385BCE)

As the king continued to embellish Karnak (Ipet-Sut) to his own designs, he dismantled earlier buildings and used their blocks as in-fill for the third pylon, a monumental gateway that he laid out over an earlier courtyard. Work on the pylon began some time after regnal year five, but the relief decoration on its east face was only completed later in the reign.

On the east face of Amenhotep's third pylon at Karnak this now-headless relief figure of the king (center right) can still be seen. He is shown wearing an ornate kilt and jewelry.

In an inscription Amenhotep described his pylon as "another monument made for Amun, a very great gateway before Amun-Ra, Lord of the Thrones of the Two Lands, covered in gold throughout and carved with the god's image in the likeness of a ram, inlaid with real lapis-lazuli and worked with gold and costly stones. The like had never before been made. It is paved in pure silver and its outer gate set with stelae of lapis-lazuli on each side. Its two sides reach up to the sky like the four supports of heaven. Its flagpoles reach skyward worked in gold. His majesty brought the gold for it from the land of Karoy on his first campaign of victory of slaying vile Kush."

The king ordered a new barque for Amun's cult statue, in which the statue could be taken out in procession and across the Nile to the West Bank. An inscription on a stela at his Kom el-Hetan funerary temple states that he made it "of new cedar wood cut on my orders in Lebanon and dragged from the mountains of Retenu by the chiefs of all foreign lands. It is very great and wide and its like has never been made before. It is lined with pure silver and worked throughout with gold, and is filled with a great shrine of gold ... It is entirely beautiful. The souls of Buto hail it and the souls of Nekhen praise it and the divine songstresses sing of its beauty. It makes the waters glitter like Aten in the sky when it makes its crossing at the Festival of Opet, at its crossing to the west of millions of years [the Theban West Bank]."

Around this time changes were becoming perceptible in royal art, particularly as the style used in portraits of Amenhotep gradually began to distinguish itself from the style that had predominated under his father, Tuthmosis IV. Although the artists and craftsmen responsible for Egypt's magnificent artistic legacy did not sign their work and therefore remain largely unknown, those who produced much of the superb material that survived from Amenhotep III's reign are, exceptionally, known by name.

Countless numbers of skilled craftsmen were employed to beautify the temple of Karnak and Amenhotep's other building projects. In this fragment of a painted tomb scene, a rather unkempt carpenter is portrayed hard at work.

The twin brothers Suti and Hor were architects holding the title "overseer of the works of Amun" under Amenhotep III. Describing the work they did at the temples of Karnak (see pages 40–41) and Luxor (see pages 114–117) on a stela containing an early hymn to the Aten, the twins spoke to Amun with one voice: "I was overseer of works in your very shrine made for you by your beloved son Nebmaatra, given life ... But my brother, my image, I trust his ways, he came out of the womb with me on the same day. In Southern Ipet [Luxor] when I was in charge on the west side he was in charge on the east side. We controlled the great monuments of Ipet-Sut at the front end of Thebes in the city of Amun."

The title "master of works and chief sculptor" was held by the official Men, followed by his son Bek, who served Amenhotep's successor, Akhenaten. Men was shown on a rock stela at Aswan making offerings to Amenhotep III's statue "king of kings, lord of might"—one of the two Colossi of Memnon figures whose construction he oversaw later in the reign (see page 142). Another of Amenhotep's officials, named Huy, referred to himself as a "sculptor of Amun" in his Theban tomb inscriptions.

SON OF THE GODS

YEARS 8–9 (ca. 1384–1383BCE)

At el-Riziquat (Sumenu), Amenhotep erected a great temple in honor of the crocodile god Sobek, who was revered as "lord of Bakhu," the horizon. A superb statue group depicts the enthroned and elaborately crowned crocodile-headed god embracing the standing figure of the king (see right). Increasingly Amenhotep sought to emphasize connections between the gods and the royal throne. Certain divinities, such as Ra, Sobek, Hathor, and the sky goddess Nut, seem to have been particularly important to him. By associating himself with them, he could express royal power and attributes.

Items such as this 18th-Dynasty "swimming-girl" wooden spoon may have had a ritual as well as a cosmetic purpose. The female figure that forms the handle of this spoon has recently been interpreted as representing the sky goddess Nut.

Amenhotep ordered countless statues to be raised in tribute to the gods and goddesses, bringing honor to his name by linking it with theirs: the statues bore inscriptions naming the king as "Nebmaatra, beloved of" the god represented, establishing the king's divinely ordained status. He had them placed in temples throughout the empire alongside his own statuary, intending the gods and goddesses to be seen as one and the same with the king their son represented as one of them.

In this way Amenhotep cast himself as a member of the family of deities, and the connection was further emphasized by the fact that the figures all shared the characteristic facial features of the king—stressing in concrete

This lifesize alabaster (calcite) dyad represents the crocodile god Sobek, embracing Amenhotep III in a paternal gesture while holding the *ankh* sign—the breath of life—to the king's face.

fashion the intimate relationship between the ruler and his divine mothers and fathers. The accompanying text reinforced the visual message, sometimes describing the king as existing in "the image of" this or that deity.

Amenhotep fitted the gods' beautifully decorated temples with all manner of ritual furniture and equipment, together with the means to produce the offerings they required. As a dutiful son, the king proved himself incredibly generous to his divine parents and, in making offerings to the great Amun,

One of Amenhotep's favorite deities was Thoth, represented in this quartzite statue in the form of a baboon. The god is portrayed in a seated posture, ready to greet the rising sun.

he was able to claim that "I have assigned to him thousands of cattle so as to provide choice cuts of meat." At Karnak, Amenhotep honored Amun as Amun-Ra, the god's statuary reflecting the benign royal features.

In Heliopolis the high priests of Ra served the sun god, while in the traditional capital Memphis the high priests of Ptah, "lord of *maat*, the fair of face," oversaw the cult of the creator god whom the king sought to emulate in his vast building projects. Four monumental quartzite figures of Thoth, set up at his cult center of Hermopolis (Ashmunein), bore witness to Amenhotep's devotion to the god of wisdom and writing. Thoth's figures took the form of the potentially aggressive baboon, a cult animal which was associated with the rising sun and solar worship but which also had lunar connections when associated with Thoth.

As he emphasized the gods' links to the sun and to his own throne, Amenhotep adopted a newly systematic approach to the myriad divinities of the Egyptian pantheon, establishing more clearly the individual deities' roles and characteristics. In addition to the great gods of state worshiped in grand temples throughout the empire, less formal representations of protective household deities were made in profusion, adorning palace walls, household furniture, and cosmetic items. Images of the dwarf god Bes and the hippopotamus goddess Taweret were particularly popular.

One of the most striking features of Amenhotep's reign was the king's devotion to female divinity and the large number of female images produced. The basic element of royal power was the right to rule, symbolized by the goddess Maat, daughter of the sun god and personification of order and harmony. In images the king appears repeatedly in female company, surrounded by his female relations and women of his court—the male element at the center of a female world.

The protection afforded by women reflected that offered by the Two Ladies, the vulture goddess Nekhbet and the cobra goddess Wadjet, who had strong solar connections and were believed to guard the king at all times. The greatest goddess of Amenhotep's reign, however, was Hathor, goddess of love. Her image was bound up with that of the sun god himself. She was his mother, wife, and daughter and was also the god's protector when she became the Eye of Ra. Her name, "Hat-Hor" or "Huwt-Hor," actually means "house of Horus" and can be interpreted as the womb that surrounded the king in his aspect as an embodiment of Horus.

Although most often portrayed in her nurturing form as a beautiful woman or benevolent bovine figure, Hathor also had a destructive side. Her vengeful quality was personified by the lioness goddess Sekhmet. The ancient Egyptians recognized the female capacity for aggression and violence when threatened, and Sekhmet, "the powerful one," was the bloodthirsty bringer of destruction—a mighty goddess of war who represented the pharaoh's great prowess in battle. In her lioness form Hathor-Sekhmet was believed once to have unleashed a savage assault on humankind on behalf of Ra, who was angered by humans' lack of respect for him. It was from the aggressive vitality of the goddess that the monarch drew his strength and powers of dynamic leadership.

It has been estimated that in the course of his reign Amenhotep set up hundreds of black-granite statues of the goddess Sekhmet around Karnak's Mut temple and his own funerary temple at Kom el-Hetan on the Theban West Bank. The statues may have been intended to form a giant calendar, with a different statue honored every day and each one representing one of the 365 different aspects of the goddess. The king also erected black-granite figures representing the goddesses Isis and Nephthys—protectors of their brother Osiris and defenders of the sun god on his nightly journey through the darkness of the underworld—in addition to figures of Neith, another warrior goddess, "mistress of the bow, ruler of the arrows."

The sky goddess Nut was a popular figure in smaller-scale representations. They took the form of the celebrated "swimming-girl spoons" (see illustration, page 56), the handles of which represent an outstretched, naked female body. The spoons have long been regarded as nothing more than charming cosmetic objects, but recent reinterpretation has suggested that the female figure on the handle depicts the great sky goddess herself, whose body, stretched out across the heavens in the same way that she appeared on coffin lids and tomb ceilings, arched over the deceased in order to restore them to life.

The name of Amenhotep III is inscribed on this bronze counterpoise from a *menat*— a large beaded collar worn or carried by priestesses of Hathor. Below the pharaoh's cartouche are representations of the goddess in her bovine form and a reference to her epithet, "the Golden One."

HAIL TO THE ATEN

In a continuation of his father's policy, Amenhotep focused the religious ideology of his court increasingly on solar worship. The period in which the state god Amun was united with the sun god to create Egypt's ultimate deity, Amun-Ra, saw the solar image achieve ever-greater prominence in the form of the Aten (the sun disk that was now worshiped as a god).

The Aten was first referred to during the Middle Kingdom ca. 1950BCE, and the living king was likened to the Aten as early as the first years of the Eighteenth Dynasty. The Aten's earliest representation in its familiar form of a disk adorned with the royal uraeus serpent, and rays ending in small hands holding out the *ankh* sign, appeared on a stela erected at Giza by Amenhotep II, Amenhotep III's grandfather. Amenhotep II's son, Tuthmosis IV, was identified in his inscriptions as "lord of what the Aten encircles" (see page 16), and it was the Aten, rather than the god Amun, that appeared in

This pectoral ornament (which was designed to be worn on the chest) was found in the Theban tomb of Hatiay, the granary overseer of the royal "mansion of the Aten." The pectoral is made of wood overlaid with gold. On the reverse (shown here) the base of the inset scarab is flanked by the keeling figures of the protective goddesses Isis and Nephthys.

one of the inscriptions referring to Tuthmosis's military conquests. Throughout his reign Tuthmosis stressed his allegiance to the sun god rather than solely to Amun—a religious policy later developed and pursued by his son Amenhotep III.

Through his choice of names and epithets, Amenhotep III publicly announced his solar allegiance, proudly and repeatedly confirming that he was the sun god's chosen one and the one made in that god's image. A favourite appellation of the king was "Aten-Tjehen," which literally means "the dazzling sun disk." The term was also used for a company of royal troops and for the state barge, the *Aten-Tjehen*, which was moored in front of the royal palace at Thebes (see pages 128–133). The palace was itself called "Splendor of the Aten."

During Amenhotep's reign, moreover, there appeared the first evidence of an actual cult of the Aten, which was based at Heliopolis in Lower Egypt and had its own temple and priesthood. The northern vizier Aper-el was appointed its high priest, while the official Ramose (see page 103) was appointed "steward in the mansion of the Aten," in which the scribe Hatiay was "overseer of the granaries."

The sun god was increasingly praised throughout Egypt. Even the celebrated "Hymn to the Aten," dating from the reign of Amenhotep's successor, Akhenaten, was anticipated in an earlier hymn of praise found on the stela of Amenhotep III's architects, the twins Suti and Hor. Their hymn ran as follows. "Hail to you, Aten of daytime, Creator of all who makes all things live! ... Creator of the earth's bounty, Khnum and Amun of humankind, who seized the Two Lands from great to small, kindly mother of the gods and humans, the craftsman with a patient heart ... The shepherd who drives his flock, their refuge made to sustain them ... Khepri of noble birth, who raises his beauty within Nut's body, who lights the Two Lands with his light. Oldest one of the Two Lands, he who made himself, who sees all that he made, he alone ... Rising in heaven formed as Ra, he makes seasons with the months, heat as he desires, cold as he desires, he takes bodies and embraces them, every land rejoicing at his rising and every day giving praise to him."

The importance of the Aten grew throughout Amenhotep III's long reign. In the last decade of his rule the king even officially identified himself as the sun god the Aten (see page 154).

THE FIERCE-EYED LION

YEAR 10 (ca. 1382BCE)

Amenhotep marked the tenth anniversary of his accession by issuing two commemorative scarabs. The king's grip on Egypt's empire was so firm that he had few military exploits to boast of. Instead, the first scarab praised his great skill as a hunter of lions. The second scarab announced an important international and personal event: Amenhotep's marriage to Princess Kiluhepa, the daughter of King Shuttarna II, who ruled the powerful Syrian state of Mitanni. She was to be the first of many foreign brides, and arrived in Egypt with a retinue of 317 women—"a marvel," according to her new husband.

The "Lion Hunt" scarab records the 102 lions killed by Amenhotep during the first ten years of the reign, so demonstrating the king's peerless strength and bravery. Given Egypt's might, the scarab establishes Amenhotep III's prowess at a time when there were simply no more battles to be fought. Lion hunting was a favorite royal pursuit and the animals were even kept as royal pets during the later New Kingdom.

The "Lion Hunt" scarab has survived in profusion—123 examples have been found in Egypt and elsewhere. Archaeologists have discovered examples of the scarab as far afield as Lachish (on the coast of the Levant in modern Lebanon) and even beyond the empire on the island of Cyprus. Its reference to the king's "own arrows" underlines Amenhotep's great love of archery; his wristguard, used for self-protection when firing arrows, has survived and was made of finely worked red leather (see page 38). The lion

was a widely used symbol of kingship: Amenhotep himself was described in several inscriptions as "Nebmaatra, the fierce-eyed lion," "mighty lion," and "lion of rulers." The king was also portrayed in various temple and palace reliefs as a sphinx—the human-headed lion of mythology—trampling his enemies. Other representations of him in sphinx form range from monumental sculpted figures in red granite and sandstone to smaller figures made of faience. One later cartoon scene in a satirical papyrus shows a lion playing the board game senet with a small gazelle (see page 28), an image scholars often interpret as representing a pharaoh at leisure with a graceful woman of his harem. Images of lions were used as a popular decorative motif on a wide range of items, from cosmetic pots and votive objects to jewelry and furniture, and were greatly treasured as protective devices.

Lions were also regarded as solar creatures in Egyptian tradition: because they lived on the edge of the desert they were believed to be guardians of the horizon at the places where the sun rose and set. The lion god Aker supposedly guarded the western and eastern edges of the underworld—the entrance to and exit from the realm through which the sun

One of a pair of monumental red-granite lions that once guarded the temple of Soleb in the Sudan. Erected by Amenhotep III, they were dedicated to his deified self as Nebmaatra, lord of Nubia.

Like his grandfather before him, Amenhotep III was a skilled charioteer and archer. This image, from a stela from his funerary temple, shows him driving his chariot, armed with bow and arrows. On the backs of the horses are four bound Nubian captives; two others, just visible here, are being trampled under the wheels of the king's chariot.

passed each night. Aker was often represented in the form of two lions positioned back to back so that one faced sunset and the other sunrise; they were known as the lions of "yesterday" and "tomorrow." The sun itself was sometimes represented in feline form as the "lion of Ra."

In contrast with the ubiquitous "Lion Hunt" scarab, only five copies have survived of the scarab that proclaimed the king's marriage to Princess Kiluhepa (see box below). Friendly relations with Mitanni had previously been sealed by Tuthmosis IV's marriage to a daughter of the Mitannian king Artatama I and Amenhotep followed enthusiastically his father's policy of diplomacy by marriage.

After Amenhotep's marriage to Kiluhepa, the princess's brother Tushratta acceded to the Mitannian throne. Tushratta wrote to his brother-in-law Amenhotep, calling him "Nibmuareya," the Mitannian form of the Egyptian king's title "Nebmaatra." In his letter (see box opposite) Tushratta explained the earlier political unrest in Mitanni and proclaimed his desire to continue the mutually beneficial alliance between his own country and Egypt against the growing power of the Hittites in the north. He ended by mentioning the presents he was sending to the royal couple. Later in his reign Amenhotep III would take more foreign wives from Mitanni,

THE MARRIAGE OF AMENHOTEP III TO PRINCESS KILUHEPA

"Regnal year 10 under the majesty of Horus: Strong Bull, appearing in truth; He of the Two Ladies: who establishes laws and pacifies the Two Lands; Golden Horus: great of strength, smiter of the Asiatics; the king of Upper and Lower Egypt, lord of the Two Lands: Nebmaatra, chosen one of Ra, son of Ra, Amenhotep, ruler of Thebes given life, and of the great royal wife Tiy—may she live. The wonders that were brought to his majesty were the daughter of Shuttarna, king of Naharin [Mitanni], Kiluhepa, and the chief women of her harem, total: 317 women."

Arzawa (southwestern Anatolia), and Babylon. Such arrangements were not simply a matter of policy between kings who used their daughters and sisters as diplomatic pawns against the women's will—in a remarkable letter written in Babylonian script, one of the princesses professed her great devotion to her future husband (see page 146).

TUSHRATTA, KING OF MITANNI, TO AMENHOTEP III

"Say to Nibmuareya, the king of Egypt my brother: so speaks Tushratta, king of Mitanni, your brother. For me all goes well. For you may all go well. For Kiluhepa may all go well. For your household, for your wives, for your sons, for your nobles, for your warriors, for your horses, for your chariots, and in your country may all go very well. I was young when I first sat on the throne of my father, and Ud-hi had done a terrible thing to my country and slain his lord. For this reason he would not permit me friendship with anyone who loved me. I in my turn could not rest regarding the terrible things that had been done in my country and I killed the traitors who had killed my brother Artashumara and everyone belonging to them. Since you were friendly with my father I have accordingly written and told you, so that you my brother might hear these things and rejoice. My father loved you, and you in turn loved my father. In keeping with this love my father gave you my sister. And who else stood with my father as you did? When the enemy advanced against my country I defeated them and there was not one of them who returned to their country. I now send you a chariot with two horses and a male and female attendant from the land of Hatti. As a greeting gift I also send you five more chariots and five teams of horses. And as a greeting gift to my sister Kiluhepa I send her a set of gold brooches, a pair of gold earrings, a gold ring, and a bottle of sweet perfume. I also send to you my chief minister Keliya and Tunip-ibri. May you my brother send them back quickly so that they can report back to me and bring me your greetings over which I can rejoice. May you my brother seek friendship with me and send your messengers to me so I may hear your greetings to me."

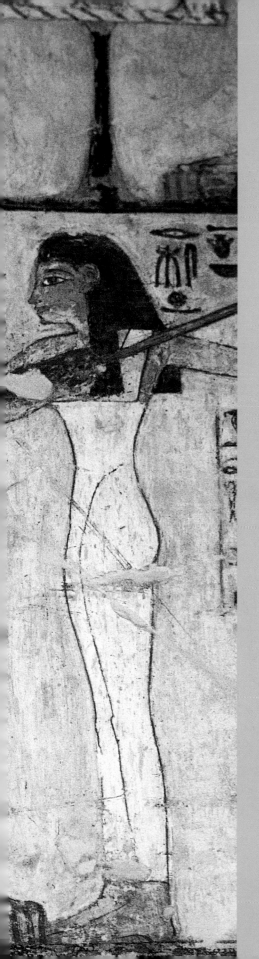

Chapter Three

AMUN IS SATISFIED

ca. 1381–1372 BCE

In this detail from the painted tomb of Rekhmire,
vizier to Amenhotep's ancestor Tuthmosis III, a
harpist sings a festive hymn to the goddess Maat.

WATER FOR THE QUEEN'S LAND

YEAR 11 (ca. 1381BCE)

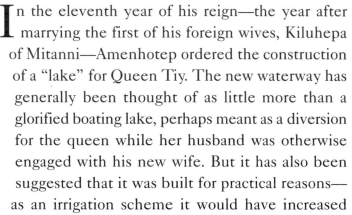

In the eleventh year of his reign—the year after marrying the first of his foreign wives, Kiluhepa of Mitanni—Amenhotep ordered the construction of a "lake" for Queen Tiy. The new waterway has generally been thought of as little more than a glorified boating lake, perhaps meant as a diversion for the queen while her husband was otherwise engaged with his new wife. But it has also been suggested that it was built for practical reasons— as an irrigation scheme it would have increased revenue on the queen's land. So Amenhotep may have undertaken the work to honor and reward his first and greatest royal wife and to provide a public sign that her supreme position as his queen could not be challenged by any foreign princess.

The great royal wife Tiy is portrayed in this small green-steatite head wearing a double uraeus and circular crown decorated with winged uraei. The piece was discovered in Hathor's temple in the Sinai.

The construction of the queen's lake is reported on the fifth and final of the commemorative scarab series. It records: "Regnal year 11 under the majesty of Horus, Strong Bull, appearing in truth, He of the Two Ladies, who establishes laws and pacifies the Two Lands; Golden Horus: great of strength, smiter of the Asiatics; king of Upper and Lower Egypt, lord of the Two Lands: Nebmaatra; son of Ra: Amenhotep, ruler of Thebes, given life; and the great royal wife Tiy, may she live. Her father's name is Yuya, her mother's name is Tuya. His majesty commanded the making of a lake for the great royal wife, may she live, in her town of Djarukha. Its length is 3,700 cubits and its width is 700 cubits. His majesty celebrated the festival of the opening of the lake in the third month of the inundation on day 16, when his majesty was rowed on it in the royal barge ... " Eleven "Lake" scarabs have survived, but only this one also refers to Tiy's parentage.

The mention of "Djarukha"—an otherwise unknown location—seems most likely to be a reference to Tiy's family town of Akhmim. Traditionally, historians believed that the lake referred to in the scarab was built at Thebes because of the presence there of an enormous T-shaped depression in front of the royal palace. But the indentation at Thebes is now known to have been a harbor measuring 1 mile (1.6 kilometers) in width. Skillfully built to link the royal residence to the Nile, the harbor and its approach waters bore a heavy flow of commercial and administrative traffic. The Thebes harbor also provided a mooring for the great royal barge known as *The Dazzling Aten* on which Amenhotep and Queen Tiy sailed majestically forth during religious and state festivals.

This limestone relief figure of Queen Tiy was cut from the wall of the Theban tomb of Userhet, the "overseer of royal apartments." In the original scene the queen, holding her flail, was depicted sitting behind the king to receive offerings. Tiy's diadem is set with double uraei and decorated at the back with an outstretched falcon.

FROM THE PROVINCES
TO THE PALACE

RIGHT From the tomb of Amenhotep III's father-in-law Yuya and mother-in-law Tuya, in the Valley of the Kings, this detail shows Yuya's face represented on his inner gilded coffin.
BELOW Queen Tiy was often portrayed with the regalia of the goddess Hathor, pictured here wearing a crown featuring cow's horns and the solar disk.

Queen Tiy is one of the best-documented royal figures of ancient Egypt. After her marriage to the young Amenhotep III she rapidly gained great power and influence. Her name was twinned with that of her husband throughout his reign and follows that of the king on all of the five scarab series—even her parents' names are recorded on some of the scarabs, an unprecedented honor.

They wed during the king's first regnal year, at a time when neither she nor Amenhotep could have been much more than 12 years old. It is likely, therefore, that the marriage was arranged by the regent, Queen Mutemwia, who may herself have come from the same family of provincial officials as the new queen. In marrying Tiy, Amenhotep broke with tradition—both his father and grandfather before him had married within the royal house.

Tiy's family came from Akhmim in Middle Egypt, between Amarna and Thebes. Her father Yuya was the royal lieutenant-commander of chariotry and held the religious title "god's father," a common office held by men ranging from viziers to tutors. He was also priest of the local Akhmim god Min, while her mother Tuya was a priestess of Min, Amun, and Hathor. Their son, Tiy's brother Anen, described himself as "one great of love in the king's house, enduring of favors in the palace." He was a hereditary noble, mayor, and seal-bearer of the king, and also served in the priesthood—in which profession he was later promoted to high office as the second prophet of Amun at the Karnak temple.

Some scholars have suggested that Tiy was not Egyptian by birth, but there is little evidence to support such a theory. One argument— that she was Nubian—was based on the supposed appearance of her parents' mummies, but these in fact display aquiline facial features and fair, Caucasian-type hair. Others claimed that Tiy was from Syria, an idea supported by one description of a celebrated carved head of the queen made from dark yew wood as having

pale skin and eyes—despite the fact that it clearly has dark irises. Furthermore, among her parents' extensive funerary equipment—which Amenhotep provided for them in a tomb in the royal necropolis in the Valley of the Kings—there were no items suggesting that the family might have had foreign origins.

Yuya's and Tuya's tomb, which was found largely intact, contained a combination of practical everyday items and stunning works of art, including golden coffins and gilded furniture, jars of perfume and a wig box, over-stuffed cushions, rows of sandals, and even bunches of vegetables. The couple's coffins are wonderfully crafted, Tuya's broad smile causing the viewer to forget entirely that the portrait is actually a death mask. Their image is also preserved in their funerary papyri, where Yuya's white hair is shown contrasting with the black tresses of his wife—although both their mummies have fair hair. The black wig discovered in the tomb indicates that the couple, like most well-to-do Egyptians, would have worn wigs at various times. The mummy of Yuya (see page 144) is regarded as the best preserved of all Egyptian mummies—Amenhotep's reign marked a high point in the art of embalming.

Amenhotep's new wife Queen Tiy became a key figure in his court. She took an active role in politics and corresponded on her own behalf with foreign dignitaries, who clearly respected her wise counsel. In addition to documentary sources, the sheer number of surviving representations of the queen indicate her great importance to the king. She provided the female element that brought vital balance to Amenhotep's role as pharaoh, and in the same way that gods' figures carry his features, so those of goddesses are shown with the features of his beloved wife.

The blue inscription on this yellow faience cosmetic pot names (left to right): "Son of Ra, Amenhotep, ruler of Thebes," "Nebmaatra the good god," and "king's wife Tiy." The lip of the pot is skillfully decorated with red, white, and green petal details.

Tiy is also shown wearing traditionally divine regalia. The horns and solar disk, tall feathers, and vulture head were incorporated into the queen's own crowns. Her stunning robe of feathers represented the plumage of the great vulture goddesses Mut and Nekhbet (see page 43). The queen was described as "great of favors, great king's wife Tiy, beloved of Nekhbet," and so was associated with the goddess who helped the sun god as he traveled through the sky, in the same way that the queen herself helped the king through his reign.

The notion of the queen as goddess can be seen as complementary to that of the king as sun god, neatly establishing Queen Tiy as Amenhotep's partner in both the divine and mortal spheres. She accompanied her husband as the earthly embodiment of Maat. Tiy was also worshiped as the incarnation of the goddess Hathor-Sekhmet in her violent aspect when she assumes the awesome power of the "Eye of Ra," the daughter and protector of the sun god with the powers of Maat: "The eye of Ra appears against you, she devours you, she punishes you," went one warning to all the pharaoh's enemies, lest they forget that at all times he was guarded by the might of his omnipresent goddess-queen. This violent aspect of Tiy as Sekhmet was reflected in unprecedented representations of the queen as a sphinx—an image that had previously been the preserve of kings alone. As sphinx, Tiy appears both crouched, guarding the royal cartouche, and rampant, trampling the enemy. The images represent the queen as the fearless defender of the pharaoh and of Egypt in the same way that the goddess defended the god.

As befitted one of her exalted status, Tiy oversaw a large household of attendants and servants who provided for her material needs. At Thebes she was served by her steward Kheruef, while later, at Amarna, Huya held the title "steward in the house of the king's mother the great royal wife Tiy." She employed her own chef, Bakenamun, and even had her own sculptor, Iuty, to fashion likenesses of her growing family. After the death of her husband, the queen moved her household to the royal palace at Gurob, where she was attended by her female staff including Lady Teye, chief of the household, the singer Mi, Tuty, and girls by the names of Nebetya and Tama—all of whom are represented in a group of skillfully carved wooden figurines that was found with the dark yew-wood head that portrays Queen Tiy herself.

Made of Cypriot yew wood, this small head of Queen Tiy features ebony, obsidian, and alabaster inlays for the eyes and earrings of gold and lapis-lazuli. The queen's original silver-and-gold headcover, still visible over her brow, indicates that the head originally portrayed her as a funerary goddess to her dead husband. The present headcover of molded linen—which was once covered in tiny blue beads—was added after the Amarna Period.

THE GRIP OF EMPIRE

YEAR 12 (ca. 1380BCE)

Egyptian power reached its zenith during Amenhotep III's reign, when the king ruled over a great empire. By the twelfth year of his rule Amenhotep was already in a strong military position, for he had complete domination of Nubia, thanks to his victorious campaign there seven years earlier, and peace held in the Near East. He enjoyed warm relations with the Mitannians, and the Assyrians, Babylonians, and Hittites posed no threat to his power. Amenhotep also maintained a firm grip over the Asiatic vassal states, which provided a buffer zone against more distant threats and were a rich source of tribute.

The vassal states were divided into three administrative areas, each with an Egyptian governor as an "overseer of northern countries." The governor based at Gaza was responsible for "Canaan" (Palestine and the Phoenician coast up to Beirut), while the governor at Kumidu (Lebanon) was in charge of "Apu" (stretching inland to Syria and including Damascus). A third governor in Simurru (Syria) was responsible for "Amurru" (encompassing land along the coast as far north as Ugarit).

The governors' role was to ensure that leaders of the vassal states—men such as Ribb-Adda of Byblos and Abdi-Ashirta of Amurru—were obedient. Vassal leaders were permitted to remain in place to administer their lands, provided they remained loyal to Egypt. In return they were required to make regular annual tribute—consisting mainly of wood, metal, manufactured goods, livestock, and manpower—and were expected to supply the Egyptian military garrisons stationed in their localities. Garrisons were established inland at Beth Shan and Kumidi and on the coast at Jaffa, Gaza, Sumur, and Ullaza—locations chosen to safeguard all-important trade links. With the memory of Egyptian conquests still fresh in the minds of the local populace, even modest-sized garrisons acted as a strong deterrent against rebellion. From time to time local vassal rulers even requested that the king send extra troops to provide protection in quarrels between neighbors. The rivalry between Amurru and Byblos was highlighted in diplomatic correspondence when both vassals wrote separately to Egypt, each asking for help against the other.

The many artifacts bearing Amenhotep's name that have been found across western Asia attest to Egyptian activity there at this time. Moreover, inscriptions on statue bases from the king's funerary temple at Kom el-Hetan even claim dominion over the Aegean—including Mycenae, Troy, and Knossos, familiar names from ancient Greek history that first appear in Egyptian records during Amenhotep's reign. The extent of Amenhotep's actual political power in the Aegean was limited, although his name was certainly known as far afield as Mycenae, where his cartouche has been found. One of the Kom el-Hetan inscriptions claims the pharaoh's supremacy over the entire world: "All countries of the Phoenicians and the north and the south are under the feet of this good god. The princes of all northern and all southern countries come on their knees, united in one place, that the breath of life be given to them by the king."

In a painted scene from the Theban tomb of the treasurer Sobekhotep, Syrian tribute-bearers are shown arriving at the Egyptian court with gifts for the king. They are accompanied by the child of one of the vassal rulers (upper register, center). Such children were often brought up in Egypt, both to guarantee their fathers' obedience and to give them an Egyptian education.

PAX AMENOPHICA:
PEACE AND PLENTY

YEAR 13 (ca. 1379BCE)

By the thirteenth year of the reign, with Nubia stabilized and the vast empire at peace, Egypt was at the height of its wealth and power. The rule of Amenhotep III saw four decades of prosperity uninterrupted by war; for the people of Egypt it was a time of unparalleled security and optimism—a golden age presided over by a golden king. To Amenhotep's grateful subjects it must have seemed that his success proved that he was at one with the gods themselves.

At this time Egypt had a population estimated at between three and four million, almost all living on the fertile banks of the River Nile bordered by barren desert. The traditional administrative capital was Memphis, at the apex of the Delta in Lower Egypt. However, Thebes in Upper Egypt was the country's greatest city and religious capital, the home of the state god Amun-Ra and burial place of Amenhotep's Eighteenth-Dynasty predecessors. Filled with the funerary temples of these dead pharaohs, Thebes's West Bank was also home to royal tombs and the burials of the kings' subjects, while on the East Bank stood the city of the living and the temples of their gods. Known simply as "The City," or *Waset* (meaning "scepter"), Thebes was a noisy, sprawling metropolis, whose great gold-covered state buildings could be seen for miles around. Its reputation spread throughout the ancient world; around the ninth century BCE the Greek poet Homer, in his *Iliad*, hailed it as "hundred-gated Thebes" on account of its many temple pylons.

The city's sophisticated and worldly population enjoyed a standard of living unsurpassed elsewhere in Egypt, and the élite developed a new taste for luxury and refinement as a result of the endless stream of exotic goods pouring into the country from across their vast empire; many of these imports are listed and described in contemporary diplomatic correspondence. At the same time, home-produced goods began to reveal foreign influence, as Egyptian tastes became truly cosmopolitan.

During his long reign Amenhotep progressively remodeled and realigned much of Thebes. As the number of royal and religious structures there increased, so too did the number of administrative and domestic buildings needed to house the growing army of officials. The wealthiest of these officials lived in multistoried town houses or on country estates provided by the king. At the heart of each estate stood a large villa, set in a walled garden, with a tree-lined pool full of fish, ducks, and lotus flowers. The ancient Egyptians' passionate regard for their gardens is well attested: the writer of one contemporary love poem said that "I belong to you like this garden that I planted with flowers and sweet-smelling plants."

Like all Egyptian houses, these villas would have been made of mud-bricks, often stamped with the royal cartouche and painted white on the outside to reflect the heat. The temperature inside each house was kept to a minimum by making the windows small and setting them high up in the walls to catch any breezes. The villas' interiors were beautifully decorated in the naturalistic artistic style made popular by the royal court: the walls were freely painted with plants and animals; the floors were covered with bright, glazed tiles depicting flowers, birds, and animals; and the king's name was displayed around the house as a good-luck charm. The remains of even modest homes of the time reveal traces of brightly colored wallpaintings.

A typical villa could have up to 30 or 40 rooms, including pillared halls and reception rooms, a dining room, and a household shrine for small figures of the gods, the royal family, and family ancestors. There were bedrooms and guest quarters, and even limestone-lined bathrooms laid out en suite. In a story from an earlier time, the house of a prince was described as having "a bathroom with mirrors," while ancient Egyptian bath

This elaborate jewel casket was found in the tomb of Yuya and Tuya, Queen Tiy's parents. The casket is made of gilded wood, faience, and ivory. It is decorated with the name of the queen and those of Amenhotep III, as well as repeated *ankh*, *was*, and *neb* signs, meaning "all life and power."

towels, with their looped threads, have a strikingly modern appearance. As today in Egypt, houses had stairs to a flat roof terrace, where the family could sleep or sit beneath a shaded pavilion and enjoy the cool breezes from the river. Close to the house would be the kitchens, storerooms, and granaries.

Guests and family alike would have enjoyed the use of beautifully made furniture—surviving examples from Amenhotep's reign include wooden chairs and stools, couches, and beds. Rooms would have been adorned with wallhangings and feather-stuffed cushions, and would have contained chests and boxes for storage, together with a whole range of cosmetic and perfume vessels. After dark, the villa's inhabitants used lamps—pottery bowls of oil with linen wicks—to provide light, as well as candles, which were sometimes colored and scented.

Although houses were not overcluttered with ornamentation, flowers seem to have been extremely popular in all homes—in vases, bowls, or bouquets, "all the good things that sprout from the earth are good things

From the Theban tomb of Nebamun, this fragment of a painted wall scene shows the wealthy scribe's beautiful garden. It is typical of the nobility's gardens of the period, with its lotus pool surrounded by date palms and sycamore figs. Sophisticated irrigation systems were required to sustain such lush gardens in the arid Egyptian climate.

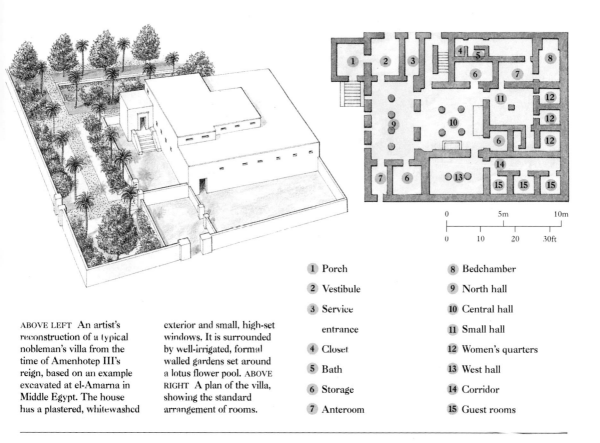

ABOVE LEFT An artist's reconstruction of a typical nobleman's villa from the time of Amenhotep III's reign, based on an example excavated at el-Amarna in Middle Egypt. The house has a plastered, whitewashed exterior and small, high-set windows. It is surrounded by well-irrigated, formal walled gardens set around a lotus flower pool. ABOVE RIGHT A plan of the villa, showing the standard arrangement of rooms.

1 Porch
2 Vestibule
3 Service entrance
4 Closet
5 Bath
6 Storage
7 Anteroom

8 Bedchamber
9 North hall
10 Central hall
11 Small hall
12 Women's quarters
13 West hall
14 Corridor
15 Guest rooms

strewn about the house"—as a hymn to the Nile-god Hapy stated. The Egyptians also kept lists of "substances in order to make pleasant the smell of the house or clothes: myrrh, frankincense, cyperus grass—crush, grind, make into one and burn on the fire." One story told of a house "scented with incense put on the brazier," while another said a house contained "choice perfumes in every room."

Wealthy families would keep a large staff of servants to care for them. These often included a butler, secretary, cook, laundryman, hairdresser, watchman, gardener, stablehand, childrens' nurse, maids, and attendants—each with their own quarters. The number of servants depended on the status of the family they served.

Thebes was also home to thousands of craftsmen and workers. A number of "servants of the place of truth" (see page 90), who were devoted to the construction of the royal tombs, lived in the village of Deir el-Medina on the West Bank. In Amenhotep's day the village contained about 50 modestly sized houses with brightly painted walls and sparsely furnished interiors.

FASHION AND FINERY

This portrait of the lady Thepu is from her son Nebamun's Theban tomb. Thepu is shown wearing a full wig, a finely pleated linen dress, and colorful beaded gold jewelry. The *menat* counterpoise she holds in her hand indicates that she was a devotee of the goddess Hathor.

In court circles, men and women adorned themselves in fine linens embellished with gold and semi-precious stones, wore elaborately styled wigs, and made lavish use of cosmetics and perfumes that added to the dazzling overall effect. The opulence of this style contrasted sharply with the relative conservatism of early and mid-Eighteenth-Dynasty dress, as many exotic new fashions swept into Egypt from across the empire during Amenhotep's reign.

Amenhotep III was the first king to wear a combination of a fringed, ankle-length tunic and a pleated and fringed overgarment that covered the left arm and was knotted below the right breast, as portrayed in his statuary. Only fragments of textiles have survived from Amenhotep's reign, but at least 18 royal tunics found in the tomb of his grandson Tutankhamun provide concrete evidence of the ceremonial costume worn by late Eighteenth-Dynasty pharaohs. Among them was the so-called "falcon" tunic, featuring a pattern of rosettes in red and blue on a darker blue background, and two rows of tapestry-woven hieroglyphs down the front, which proclaimed the king to be "protector of the Two Lands" and "vanquisher of all the foes of Egypt."

Ceremonial dress worn by royal women was also highly ornate. Queen Tiy's feather dress (see page 43) was an elegant creation of feathers molded to her body: two vulture wings wrapped protectively around her hips and thighs to emphasize her role as mother, while the dress was belted tightly at the waist and held in place by wide straps over the shoulders. Most women wore wraparound dresses made from lengths of linen, similar to a modern sari. More complex versions, made of one or two lengths of cloth knotted or tucked in place, were sometimes worn. The stunning effect of such clothing is captured in Theban tomb scenes showing female figures whose bodies are still partly visible beneath layers of semitransparent pleating (as above).

Linen, the basis of all ancient Egyptian clothing, ranged from ordinary fabric to best-quality *byssos*, a gauze-like material that was reserved for the royal family and élite. The effect of *byssos* was alluded to in New Kingdom poetry: "Oh, how I love to bathe before you, allowing you to see my beauty in a dress of finest linen, wet and drenched in perfume. I go down to the water to be with you. Come, look at me."

The basic item of men's dress was the linen loincloth. Fifty examples were found in the Deir el-Medina tomb of Kha, Amenhotep's foreman, and no fewer than 145 were discovered in the tomb of Tutankhamun. More hardwearing loincloths of pierced gazelle skin were also worn during this period, mainly by military personnel. Basic linen kilts and skirts were common items, worn by both men and women, although men's kilts were usually the more elaborate, cut in varying lengths and often partly pleated with a starched front section. They sometimes incorporated a decorative sash—sash-kilts were often worn over

Tutankhamun's falcon pectoral is made of gold set with lapis-lazuli, cornelian, and colored glass.

JEWELRY

Men and women wore jewelry both for display and as protective amulets. Most necklaces contained beads made of semiprecious stones, faience, or glass, from which small figures symbolizing gods, animals, or flowers were suspended.

Rings were made in solid gold for the very wealthy and also mass-produced in faience for the less well-off. Although most faience rings were blue, examples in purple, green, and yellow have also been discovered.

Many rings carried amuletic images representing the name of the owner or that of the king—the name of Amenhotep III

was worn as a talisman by his subjects. People also wore small scarabs on their fingers, strung on a cord or metal wire—the bezels were sometimes designed to swivel so that they could also be used as seals. One beautiful example, made of silver and

steatite, names Amenhotep on one side and turns around to reveal the name of Queen Tiy inscribed on the other.

As Egyptian society grew increasingly cosmopolitan during the Eighteenth Dynasty, earrings, or *shaqyu*, became popular. They usually took the form of glass studs, glass drops, or plain rings of bronze, silver, or gold, sometimes featuring details such as the uraeus serpent, spirals, or flowers. A wide range of golden adornments such as tubes, rosettes, birds, and fish were also made to decorate the hair.

It is thought that this large faience armlet in cobalt blue—Amenhotep's favorite color—may have originally come from the king's tomb.

a loose tunic. Both men and women wore richly decorated belts and girdles over their clothes.

Full-length linen garments were worn by both sexes, with one design, known as the bag-tunic, worn largely by men. Made from a long rectangle of linen, folded in half and sewn up at the sides, the bag-tunic had openings at the top for the armholes, and a hole for the head cut out in the center and done up with two small string ties. Most surviving examples are plain, although some are dyed with natural pigments or have colored bands sewn on to or woven into the cloth.

Clothing occasionally featured detachable sleeves for the arms. In addition there were also "sleeves" for the legs: linen leggings made to tie around the legs with a V-shaped notch at the bottom end for the foot. Gloves were depicted in tomb scenes and 20 pairs were found in Tutankhamun's tomb, together with gauntlets made from thick layers of cloth with a soft lining. Recent research on the mass of linen clothing found in the tomb of Tutankhamun has even revealed the earliest Egyptian socks.

The most common form of footwear in ancient Egypt was the sandal, which was generally made of palm leaf, grass, papyrus, or leather. Those worn by the wealthy were usually decorated with gold leaf, embroidery, and beadwork. Sandals were not worn in the presence of a superior, so nobles at court would have removed them in the presence of the royal family. The soles of Amenhotep's sandals were often decorated with the figures of his enemies so that the mighty pharaoh could crush them at his every step.

Wigs were very popular in Egypt. In the north African climate, a shaven head was the coolest and most hygienic option, with the head and neck covered by a wig that allowed the heat to escape through its open-mesh base. At court highly ornate hair and wig styles developed as a sign of status as well as a means of adornment. Figures of the king occasionally feature long, straight hair, but his usual choice of wig was the short, round style or a variant with layered fringing. Most images of men show a shoulder-length "double style" achieved with a wig.

Representations of women convey a subtle erotic message, with hair hanging alluringly over the eyes or spilling down over both shoulders in a visual reference to Hathor, the goddess of love and beauty sometimes called "she of the beautiful hair." The most popular fashion for women was a voluminous, enveloping style that hid the upper body in a mass of thick hair.

A favorite of Queen Tiy, it was a style almost always achieved by artifice, in the form of either separate hair extensions or a whole wig. Men and women often enhanced their own locks with false braids. In one contemporary love poem a woman exclaims: "My heart is once again filled by your love when only part of my hair is braided ... So I'll trouble myself no longer over my hair-dressing and put on a wig to be ready at once." Wigs, such as that of Kha's wife Meryt, which was found in her tomb inside its own box, were often very elaborate. Meryt's wig featured a three-strand braid at the back—seen often in both sculpture and painted scenes—which may identify the wearer as a devotee of the goddess Hathor. Children, including the infant Amenhotep and one of his daughters, Isis, were portrayed with the characteristic sidelock.

Both hair and skin were protected from the sun by a daily application of moisturizing oil, used by all Egyptians but especially necessary for those who worked outside. Castor was the most common type of oil, although the more costly sesame, olive, safflower, moringa, linseed, and almond oils were also

In this detail of the limestone reliefs in the tomb of Ramose, the brother of the deceased (named Amenhotep) is depicted with his wife May. Amenhotep is shown wearing an intricate double wig, two gold *shebyu* necklaces, and a wide collar. May wears a full wig of carefully crimped braids (decorated with a floral headband and lotus buds), a wide collar, and a fine linen robe.

This delicate 18th-Dynasty necklace, found in Thebes, is composed of cornflower pendants and beads made of gold, cornelian, red jasper, glass, and glazed compositions.

used, as was purified, sweetened animal fat. All of these could be enhanced by the addition of perfumes extracted from flowers, herbs, and spices. Used in daily life as well as in temple and funerary rituals, Egyptian perfumes were renowned throughout the ancient world for their strength and quality.

Both women and men used cosmetics on a daily basis. Eyepaint made the eyes appear larger and more luminous; as one love poem states, "My desire for you is my eyepaint, when I see you my eyes shine." Eyepaint also had practical benefits: its application around the delicate eye area reduced the glare of the sun, its antiseptic qualities provided relief from eye complaints aggravated by sandstorms, and it helped to ward off flies. Almost everyone wore eyepaint—even tomb-builders are depicted having their eyes made up by a colleague while they take a break from work. Green copper oxide malachite was obtained from Sinai and the Eastern Desert, whereas the more familiar black kohl, made from the lead ore galena, was brought from Aswan in the south of Egypt, and the Red Sea coast. Black and green eyepaints were initially worn together, but by Amenhotep's reign Egyptians used black eyepaint on its own to produce the beautiful almond-shaped eyes seen repeatedly in ancient Egyptian art.

Women colored their lips and cheeks using ground-up red ochre, and sometimes chose tattooing as a more permanent form of self-adornment. In this period the traditional dotted patterns used across the breasts and abdomen were superseded by figures of the god Bes, placed one on each thigh. Once believed to be the mark of the prostitute, such tattoos are actually amuletic devices connected with childbirth.

Female make-up artists were employed by wealthy households, but most people would either have relied upon family or friends to help them

A TASTE OF THE EXOTIC

■ ■ ■ ■ ■ ■ ■ ■ ■ ■

Diplomatic correspondence reveals the kind of clothing and jewelry sent to Egypt from abroad. Tushratta of the Mitanni sent an inventory listing the gifts he sent to Amenhotep on the occasion of his marriage to Tushratta's daughter Taduhepa. They included: "multicolored shirts, a pair of gloves trimmed with red wool, one pair of leather shoes studded with gold ornamentation, with buttons of hiliba stone and lapis-lazuli decoration set here and there. Thirteen shekels of gold have been used on them. Also four pairs of leggings made of shaggy wool. A pair of 'betatu' shoes with rich gold decoration, six shekels of gold used on these. One pair of shoes of purple wool decorated with gold and hiliba-stone buttons and lapis-lazuli inlays in the center. Four shekels of gold have been used on these. Two pairs of shoes of colored linen. One garment of purple wool, and a pair of shirts, Hurrian-style, for the city. One city shirt, Turkish style. One pair of sashes of ornamented red wool. One linen garment, Hazor style. A pair of linen shirts, Hurrian style. A city shirt of linen. A robe of linen. One garment, Hazor style. A pair of shirts, Hurrian style. One robe and a cap of purple wool. Ten bright garments, 10 pairs of shirts, Hurrian style, 10 pairs of city shirts, 10 robes, 10 pairs of boots, 10 pairs of leggings, 10 pairs of 'betatu' shoes. One loincloth of colored material."

The list also describes Mitannian jewelry sent as gifts, including "one hand bracelet of iron overlaid with gold and inlaid birds of genuine lapis-lazuli, one foot bracelet of gold, one set of genuine lapis-lazuli beads for the hand, six per string mounted on gold, and one torque-like headbinding of twisted gold." In a separate letter Tushratta referred to a necklace he sent to the king: "I send one *maninnu* necklace of genuine lapis-lazuli and gold ... may it rest on your neck for 100,000 years." A necklace matching this description was found in a later royal burial at Tanis. It is made of large gold and grey-blue lapis-lazuli beads; one of the lapis beads is bright blue, highly polished, and inscribed in cuneiform script.

apply their cosmetics, or would have put on their own using a mirror. While many Egyptians kept their make-up pots, perfume jars, combs, and razors in baskets or small boxes, the wealthy owned beautifully decorated chests with multiple compartments and pull-out drawers for separate items. The cosmetic chests of Kha and Meryt held alabaster pots of hair ointment, perfumes, razors, combs, and hairpins. Such boxes were often portrayed in tomb scenes beneath the owners' chair so that their contents were always close at hand.

OVERLEAF A detail of fashionably dressed female banquet guests from painted scenes in the tomb of the astronomer Nakht.

PREPARING FOR THE AFTERLIFE

YEARS 14–16 (ca. 1378–1376BCE)

Amenhotep III's tomb in the Western Valley—begun during the reign of his father—was now nearing completion. Extending 260 feet (80 meters) down into the limestone cliff, it is one of the largest of all Egyptian royal tombs. Its descending entry passage includes two flights of steps and a well shaft and runs for 100 feet (30 meters) before turning left at 90 degrees into a pillared hall. Two further flights of stairs lead down into an antechamber, before another 90-degree turn to the right into a second pillared hall. Steps at the far end lead into the burial chamber, which originally contained the king's 10-foot (3-meter) sarcophagus of red Aswan granite. Connected to the king's burial chamber were two similar chambers that were intended for queens Tiy and Sitamun.

The royal sarcophagus has disappeared altogether and only the badly smashed, curved-top lid survives. However, the lid is of great interest to scholars, as it is decorated with a number of innovative features. A large pair of *wedjet* eyes—usually found on the left side of the coffin—is carved on the inside of the lid where they rested above the eyes of the king's mummy and, it was believed, allowed him to see out and upward into the heavens. Beneath the right *wedjet* eye the potent spell "I have opened your eyes for you" is inscribed, while above the eyes is an image of the sky goddess Nut, who is shown for the first time in such a context with the protective wings of the vulture goddess Nekhbet. She is accompanied by the words, "Recited by Nut: 'I have come so I may stretch myself over you, so your heart might live ... I surround you, Nebmaatra, and make your eyes bright.'"

In contrast to many of the later royal tombs, much of Amenhotep's vast tomb remains undecorated. Given the amount of time available for the preparation of the tomb during the pharaoh's long reign, this was presumably intentional. Only the well shaft, the antechamber, and the king's burial chamber itself were painted—scenes from the *Amduat* (literally, "what is in the underworld": that is, funerary texts) decorate the walls of the burial chamber, while its pillars and the walls of the well shaft and antechamber bear exquisite scenes of Amenhotep in the company of the gods, led for the first time by the goddesses Hathor and Nut. They are joined by a figure of the *ka* (soul) of Amenhotep's father, Tuthmosis IV, depicted embracing his son before leading him into the afterlife. Storerooms were added to each burial chamber to contain the vital funerary equipment of the king, his wife, and their eldest daughter.

Having chosen this secluded valley as the site for his final resting place, Amenhotep used the traditional necropolis of his predecessors, the Valley of the Kings, for non-royal burials. His parents-in-law Yuya and Tuya had a fine tomb excavated near the entrance of the valley. Their superb burial equipment was found largely intact (see pages 70–71), as was that of the

In a scene from the joint Theban tomb of Amenhotep III's royal sculptors Nebamun and Ipuki, carpenters are depicted building a gilded funerary shrine of the kind found in Tutankhamun's tomb. Such shrines were set up in tombs around the sarcophagus containing the deceased's mummy. Cult statues of the gods in temples were also kept in shrines.

more modest interment of royal fan-bearer Maiherpri, who served at court. The tombs prepared for the king's mother Mutemwia and his sisters Tiaa and Amenemipet, together with those of his daughters Henuttaneb, Isis, Nebetah, and Iny and his niece Nebiu, were located somewhere in the Valley of the Queens or in the nearby Qurna necropolis, close to Malkata Palace.

Another 40 or so smaller tombs on the Theban West Bank served as the final resting places for many of Amenhotep's trusted officials and servants. The tombs' decoration was far less formal than that of the royal burial place, and traditional scenes and motifs were interpreted freely. The styles of painted decoration found in the officials' tombs reflect the artistic developments characteristic of the reign: the proportions of the human body are shortened, with a widening of the waist, chest, and thighs; female figures become more rounded and voluptuous; the quantity of hair greatly increases; and the serene facial features of the figures reflect those of the king himself.

The men who controlled the king's empire were interred at its Theban heart—Viceroy Merymose, for example, was laid to rest in his Qurnet Murai tomb with a serpentine pectoral over his heart inscribed with "a spell for preventing the heart from creating opposition against him in the necropolis,"

ROYAL TOMB-BUILDERS

The men who built the king's huge West Valley sepulcher were known as "servants of the place of truth." Overseen by their foreman, Kha, they quarried down into the face of the limestone cliff using spikes and chisels made of copper and bronze; such metals were valuable and the issue of such tools at the beginning of each shift was carefully recorded by the team's scribes.

The scribes also noted the delivery of provisions and any absentees, together with their reasons for absence—workers stayed away because of illnesses such as eye infections or scorpion bites, or because they were burying a relative or undertaking other work for a superior.

As the tomb passages extended deeper into the rock, the men worked by the light of lamps that burned oil mixed with salt to prevent smoke damage. Behind the stone-cutters came workers responsible for dressing the rough stone and plastering it ready for the draughtsmen and painters. After laying out grids of red paint to maintain correct proportions, the draughtsmen sketched the preliminary scenes in red, then made the final outlines in black. Artists then filled them in with red, blue, green, yellow, and white paint.

Tomb-builders worked for eight days and then had two rest days. They slept in a camp of dry-stone shelters that overlooked the construction site, returning to their homes in the nearby Deir el-Medina after each "week." Food was prepared and brought from the village to the workmen by their families.

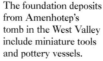

The foundation deposits from Amenhotep's tomb in the West Valley include miniature tools and pottery vessels.

his body laid within a nest of no fewer than three superbly carved granite sarcophagi. Others buried near the court they had served included Userhet, overseer of the royal apartments, Tiy's steward Kheruef ("Senaa"), and granary overseer Khaemhat ("Mahu"). Scenes of daily life captured in these men's tombs include food production. Some of the best examples are to be found in the tomb of the agricultural scribe Menna (see page 93): as well as lively portrayals of farm work, it also contains some of the most alluring female figures in the whole of ancient Egyptian art—part of the fertility imagery used throughout the tomb's decorations.

The elaborate funerary equipment placed in Egyptian tombs was meant to be used by the deceased in the afterlife. Among the objects found in the tomb of Amenhotep's foreman Kha and his wife Meryt was this painted wooden toilet ics chest containing perfume and cosmetics vessels made of glass and alabaster.

Although most officials were buried in the Theban necropolis near their king, some chose to be buried in their own locality. Many were interred in the other major burial site of Sakkara, close to the ancient capital Memphis where they had been employed. Amenhotep Huy, chief steward of Memphis, had a well-stocked tomb that included a fine quartzite canopic chest filled with human-headed jars of alabaster. Ptahmose, high priest of the Memphite god Ptah, was also buried in the great northern necropolis of Sakkara, as was the lady Henutnakhtu, and Meymery, custodian of the Memphis treasury. Meymery's tomb was decorated with finely carved reliefs portraying the tomb owner and his family enjoying their leisure and funeral scenes in which distraught mourners are shown tearing at their hair.

To the south of Thebes lay el-Riziquat (Sumenu), cult center of Sobek the crocodile god and home of a whole dynasty of treasury officials who served both the king and his father Tuthmosis. Treasury scribe Nebsen and Nebetta, the singer of Isis, seem to have been buried here, as were their daughter Hatshepsut and son-in-law Sobeknakht. The tomb of Hatshepsut's and Sobeknakht's son Sobekmose, overseer of the treasury, contains a plea to the sky goddess Nut to place the deceased among the "imperishable stars." The tomb also features a cycle of seven hymns to the sun, the moon, and various deities, in addition to superb sandstone relief scenes in which Sobekmose is depicted anointing Osiris and Anubis, the gods of the afterlife.

THE BOUNTY OF THE TWO SHORES

YEAR 17 (ca. 1375BCE)

The peaceful and prosperous Egypt of Amenhotep was blessed by good harvests and high productivity. A series of bumper crops that began at around this time continued into the latter part of his reign and was believed to be a direct result of the king's god-like ability to bring fertility to the land. The ever-increasing amounts of grain produced by the hardworking farmers were stored in new purpose-built granaries such as the great temple granary at Karnak, originally decorated with striking relief figures of the king.

As his reign progressed, Amenhotep was repeatedly portrayed in images that combined the sun's creative energies with the earth's fertility and the power of the Nile flood—all of which were bound up in the figure of Hapy, god of inundation's plenty. By the end of his reign Amenhotep is shown, rejuvenated, as Hapy, a youthful, plump, and potent god bringing wealth to his people.

In fact, the Nile's annual inundation was vital to Egypt's existence— without it the virtually rainless land would simply return to desert. The swollen Nile flooded the whole valley bottom from early September until October. After the waters had receded, a thick black silt remained to revitalize the land, in which crops were planted. Farmers also built a system of irrigation canals to extend the reach of the floodwaters and increase productivity. The crops were planted from mid-October to November and harvested the following spring (April–May); the grain was then carefully stored in granaries.

In Amenhotep's Egypt the vast majority of the population worked on the land, and in agricultural scenes the standard representations of plowing, sowing, reaping, and winnowing are often enhanced by individual portraits. As the major landowner the crown controlled the land, which was divided into estates made up of villages, their fields, and those who worked them. The official role of "overseer of the granaries of Upper and Lower Egypt" was filled by Khaemhat, among others, and he is depicted in his tomb-relief scenes proudly receiving honors from the king after a series of well-managed bumper harvests. Some lands were held by temples, through royal donation: an official named Amenhotep was "overseer of the granaries of Amun," while Hatiay was responsible for the granaries of the Aten.

The Theban tomb of Menna—the "scribe of pharaoh's fields" under Amenhotep—is richly decorated with agricultural scenes such as this one depicting the grain harvest.

A TIME OF FEASTING

YEARS 18–19 (ca. 1374–1373BCE)

The population ate well during Amenhotep's reign as rich harvests produced an abundance of grain. A staple food, grain was made into a variety of breads that were eaten by everyone together with vegetables, fruit, and beer. The wealthy supplemented their bread with meat and fine wines (a wine jar has been found in Deir el-Medina dated Year 19 of the reign), and tomb and temple scenes frequently depict foods. After Tutankhamun's funeral, guests consumed a sumptuous banquet of nine ducks, four geese, beef, lamb, and bread, accompanied by vintage wines. The remains of various food-stuffs have even been found in tombs—Kha and Meryt of Deir el-Medina were buried with a well-stocked larder.

This large pottery wine jar is in the shape of Bes, the household guardian deity associated with festivities, drunkenness, and music-making, as well as fertility.

Egyptian bakers made their bread from stoneground emmer wheat mixed with water and salt and sometimes enriched with eggs, butter, or milk. They added nuts, spices, seeds, or fruit to produce many different sweet and savory variations. Loaves were usually round, triangular, or conical, but bakers sometimes tried their hand at ornate spiral forms, and even made breads in the likeness of human or animal figures.

The ancient Egyptians ate many vegetables, including onions, leeks, garlic, beans, chickpeas, lentils, lettuce, and cucumbers. Tigernuts were popular, and almonds were found in the tombs of Tutankhamun, Kha, and Meryt at the site of Amarna. Aromatic seeds of caraway, coriander, and aniseed were used in cooking, while sesame seeds were both eaten on their own and used for oil, as were olives. Watermelons were popular, and dates, figs, pomegranates, and grapes were also eaten in large quantities and used as sweetening agents together with honey (which was obtained from both wild and domesticated bees).

The wealthy regularly ate meat—usually beef, with mutton, pork, and goat eaten more generally. Priests were allowed to consume temple offerings of animal flesh once the appetite of the gods had been sated—this would have included the pigs that Amenhotep III offered for sacrifice at the temple of Ptah in Memphis, as well as the more traditional beef. Hunters killed wild hare, gazelle, ducks, geese, quail, and pigeons for food. Fish were usually dried and salted; they formed an important part of the diet of the Deir el-Medina tomb-builders. Hens were first imported from Syria during Amenhotep's reign, while cows' milk was popular as a drink and was also used for making butter and cheese.

The richest people employed specialized cooks and kitchen staff. Queen Tiy's chef was Bakenamun, and the king's butler at Malkata was Neferronpet, "the pure of hands, great one of the chamber of the Lord of the Two Lands." Kitchens—where food was roasted, boiled, or baked using small ovens or metal braziers, or open fires—were generally set a little apart from living quarters.

Rich and poor, adults and children alike all enjoyed the standard Egyptian drink of barley beer, *henket*, which with bread formed the country's staple diet. One ritual formula states, "Give me a thousand loaves of bread and a thousand jars of beer." The beer's strength was indicated by its darkness. It seems to have been a rather thick liquid that had to be filtered before being

In this detail of a wallpainting from the tomb of the official Nakht, a servant is shown bringing geese to add to the sumptuous foodstuffs shown before him, including wildfowl and fresh fruit and vegetables.

drunk, and dates or honey were often added. A beer known as *sermet*, consumed in large quantities at Malkata, may have been enjoyed by women in particular—much of it came from the northern estates of the royal women.

The wealthy were also fond of wine, and viticulture appears in numerous tomb scenes. Egypt's best wine-producing regions were in the north, in the Delta and the oases of Kharga and Dakhla. Together with wines imported from Syria, northern Egyptian wines were brought to Thebes via Memphis. Wine was made from figs, pomegranates, and dates as well as from grapes. Another servant called Neferronpet was employed as a "supplier of sweet date wine" in Amenhotep's funerary temple. Honey and spices were sometimes added, as probably were myrrh and pistacia resins, which are natural preservatives.

Wine was called *irep*. It was labeled simply *irep*, *irep nefer* ("good wine"), *irep nefer nefer* ("very good wine") or *irep maa* ("genuine wine"). The terms *nedjem* ("sweet") and *sma* ("blended") were also used, along with the phrase "wine of becoming"—that is, still fermenting. Some labels gave the wine's purpose, from "wine for offering" and "wine for taxes" to "wine for a happy

return" and "wine for merry-making." Vintage wines were much appreciated: one wine jar in Tutankhamun's tomb was labeled "year 31" of Amenhotep's reign (ca. 1361BCE). Unlike his grandfather, Tutankhamun must have preferred dry wines: only four jars in his large collection are labeled "sweet."

In addition to large storage jars and amphorae, potters also fashioned wine jars and decanters with heads of the goddess Hathor or in the shape of Bes, the god of merry-making and guardian of wine (see page 94). People drank wine out of small bowls and stemmed goblets of glazed pottery, calcite, glass, silver, gold, or electrum. The office of royal cup-bearer at Malkata was held by the official Si-Rencnutet, also called Tjawy.

Alcohol was an important element of social and religious celebrations. Hathor was known as "lady of drunkenness" and great quantities of alcohol were consumed during her annual festival. At banquets the wine flowed freely, as indicated in Eighteenth-Dynasty tomb scenes of feasting. In one, a female guest says: "Give me eighteen cups of wine, because I want to get drunk! My insides are as dry as straw."

In this painting from his tomb at Thebes, Khaemwese (far left) oversees the production of wine, from harvesting and grape-treading to bottling.

THE KING AND THE COMMONER

O f all Amenhotep III's ministers, the closest and most important was a scribe who shared the king's name. Amenhotep "son of Hapu" rose from humble beginnings to become overseer of all Egypt's building works. After his death he even became a god and was worshiped throughout Egypt until Roman times.

Amenhotep was born to Hapu and the lady Itu ca. 1435BCE, during the reign of the warrior-pharaoh Tuthmosis III. His home was the Delta town of Athribis, to the north of modern Cairo. As a young man he was sent to the local temple school to learn the skills of the scribe—necessary for anyone seeking high office. According to the inscription on one of his statues, here he was "inducted into the gods' books [the temple library collection] and beheld the words of Thoth [hieroglyphs]; I penetrated their secrets, and learnt all their mysteries, and I was consulted on their every aspect."

At the time of Amenhotep III's accession, the son of Hapu was probably in his mid-forties. He became a royal scribe, and was also made chief priest at the local temple of Horus-Khentikheti. On another statue inscription he describes himself in typical Egyptian style as "a really excellent scribe, the first one to calculate everything."

Amenhotep son of Hapu's reputation must have reached the ear of the young king, for the official was summoned south to Thebes. Already more than 50 years old, a great age in those times, he was appointed "scribe of recruits" and made responsible for the whole of the country's manpower.

The scribe's success in this post was rewarded when he was made "overseer of all works." In this position Amenhotep son of Hapu was responsible for obtaining stone for royal monuments, including the temples of Soleb and Karnak and the massive figures of the pharaoh set up on the East and West Banks of Thebes. "I directed the king's likeness in every hard stone like heaven, directing the work of his statues, great of breadth. I did not imitate what had been done before ... and there has never been anyone who has done the same since the founding of the Two Lands."

The pharaoh made a public statement of his high regard for his overseer by ordering statues of Amenhotep son of Hapu to be placed along the processional route throughout the Karnak temple. An inscription states that the scribe would intercede with the gods themselves, on behalf of those who approached: "I am the spokesman appointed by the king to hear your words of supplication." This is another example of Amenhotep III's generosity in giving recognition to those who served him well.

The king also brought his overseer into the royal household, appointing him steward to his eldest daughter, Sitamun. The inscription on a scribal figure that portrays Amenhotep son of Hapu as an old man (see page 155) refers to this household position. It also gives the scribe's age as 80 years, adding that he hoped to reach the magical age of 110.

It is not known exactly when in Amenhotep III's reign Amenhotep son of Hapu died. His tomb was located in the Qurnet Murai hillside, near the king's funerary temple, and he was also given the unique honor of having his own funerary temple, built behind that of his monarch. In the surviving fragments of his temple's painted reliefs, the scribe wears the decorated head-band commemorating the king's jubilee celebrations, which he had been responsible for coordinating.

The scribe's fame continued to grow after his death. His funerary temple was still recognized in the Twenty-First Dynasty—more than 300 years later; and his reputation for wisdom continued into the Twenty-Second Dynasty. In this era, an inscription at Karnak hailed him: "O Amenhotep, in your great name you know the secret powers in the words of the past that date to the time of the ancestors." The cult status of Amenhotep son of Hapu culminated in his deification (see page 155), an honor first referred to during the reign of Ptolemy VI (180–164 BCE). Amenhotep III's faithful scribe was worshiped as a god in the small temple at Deir el-Medina and in the Ptolemaic chapel at Deir el-Bahari, where, 1,200 years after his death, a Greek couple named Leon and Lysandra left a dedication thanking him for the birth of their child.

Amenhotep III's favorite official, Amenhotep son of Hapu, is portrayed as a seated scribe in this black-granite statue. The text he is writing refers to the statuary of the king that he was responsible for setting up.

MASTER AND MINISTERS

Tjay was a royal scribe and "chief of the stables of pharaoh." This ebony statuette portrays the stable-master wearing a double-style wig, a finely pleated linen tunic, and four gold *shebyu* collars—badges of honor awarded by the king.

YEAR 20 (ca. 1372BCE)

In late summer ca. 1372BCE, Amenhotep and his entourage were in residence at the traditional capital, Memphis. While he was there the king appointed the official Nebnefer as "chief measurer of the granary of the god's offerings of Amun." It is revealing that more officials are known by name from the reign of Amenhotep III than from that of any other pharaoh. Their names, titles, and images have been preserved on monuments provided for them by a king who acknowledged their ability and appreciated their loyalty. At the highest level were a small group of officials handpicked by Amenhotep himself. From their achievements, it would seem that the king was a very astute judge of character.

In a Theban relief scene, Amenhotep III presides over a ceremony at which the tomb owner Khaemhat, overseer of the granaries of Upper and Lower Egypt, receives the gold *shebyu* collar of honor. His colleagues stand in rows behind him to receive similar honors, and all are anointed with great quantities of perfume. Beyond titles, gold collars, costly perfumes, and gifts inscribed with the royal name, the ultimate reward for a loyal servant of the crown was a fine tomb, designed to keep their name alive for ever. Tombs were built on the orders of the king and equiped with artifacts from the royal workshops.

Merymose shone as viceroy of Nubia for the whole of Amenhotep's reign and was honored with a nest of three royal-style sarcophagi. The location of the superbly equiped burial of the king's parents-in-law, chariotry commander Yuya and his priestess wife Tuya, in the

Valley of the Kings, is evidence of the pharaoh's desire to break with tradition by awarding trusted officials privileges that had previously been enjoyed by royalty alone.

Administrative office was often hereditary, handed down through several generations of a family that was bound to the crown by ties of loyalty and proven ability. A case in point is the Sobek family based at Sumenu, just to the south of Thebes. Nebsen served Tuthmosis IV as scribe of the treasury. Nebsen's daughter Hatshepsut and son-in-law Sobeknakht had three sons: Iuny and Huy, who both became treasury scribes, and Sobekmose, who was made "overseer of the treasury," later "overseer of works of the king in Upper and Lower Egypt" and "overseer of works in Southern Ipet" (Luxor). Sobekmose was in turn succeeded in office by his own son Sobekhotep, nicknamed "Panehesy" ("the Nubian").

However, although hereditary appointments were standard, it was possible to achieve high office through ability alone. The most impressive example of a self-made man is found in the career of the king's favorite official, Amenhotep son of Hapu, who rose from obscurity in the Delta to become overseer of all building works, and ultimately to be worshiped as a god throughout Egypt (see pages 98–99).

Some officials served several kings. For example, Horemheb, scribe of recruits, stated in his tomb inscriptions (see page 107) that he served under Amenhotep II, Tuthmosis IV, and Amenhotep III. The Deir el-Medina foreman and sculptor Kha (see page 91) also appears to have served under all three of these kings.

During Amenhotep's long reign official roles and titles changed as the civil service grew. Trusted individuals received rapid promotion and amassed an impressive array of titles. The head of the administration was traditionally the vizier, who was the king's secular deputy in the same way that the high priest represented the pharaoh in a religious capacity. The vizier—who was distinguished by his traditional dress of a long kilt, held in place by two straps, covering most of the upper as well as lower body—was involved in every aspect of government. His work was far from easy, for he was responsible for the efficient running of a vast bureaucracy. Amenhotep III's great-grandfather Tuthmosis III told his vizier: "Be watchful over your office and everything done in its name, since it supports the whole land. Indeed the office of vizier is not sweet and is truly as bitter as gall." Four viziers served

Amenhotep III: Amenhotep Huy, Aper-el, Ramose, and Ptahmose. Ramose, who also served the king's son and successor, Amenhotep IV, shared office with his colleague Ptahmose. The latter was the southern vizier during the first part of Amenhotep III's reign, having probably also served under Tuthmosis IV. A capable man, Ptahmose became incredibly powerful and bore an impressive range of titles, including "mayor of Thebes" and "overseer of all works."

The vizier worked closely with the chancellor. The latter was said to be "overseer of things that are sealed" and so was privy to confidential information. The duties of the chancellor traditionally involved organizing the expeditions sent out to obtain stone and minerals for royal projects, but Amenhotep III made this the responsibility of the overseer of the treasury. As the work entailed procuring building stone, the title "overseer of works" was added to that of treasury overseer. In Amenhotep's reign Sobekmose was noted for his success in obtaining alabaster from the quarries of Hatnub (see page 91), and his son Sobekhotep distinguished himself through his equally successful results with turquoise from Serabit el-Khadim in the Sinai (see page 158).

Egypt's main source of wealth was grain, and the role of overseer of granaries of Upper and Lower Egypt was therefore a vital one. Granary overseers were employed by the individual temples, which also had their own stewards to administer their numerous estates. The king's personal estates were maintained and managed by specially appointed stewards.

The office of scribe was the foundation of the entire administration. The great Amenhotep son of Hapu was initially a scribe. Two superb figures of Nebmerutef, royal scribe and seal-bearer and "beloved of the king," show him seated at work on a text beneath the watchful gaze of Thoth, god of learning and patron deity of scribes. The king also sent out scribes, such as May, to study places of historical interest and to undertake research into traditional practices and rituals that interested him.

The clergy was headed by the prophets of Amun, based at Karnak in the south; their power was counterbalanced by the priests of the creator god Ptah, based at Memphis in the north. The high priest of Ptah also held the title "overseer of prophets of Upper and Lower Egypt." In addition every temple in Egypt had its own high priest, wielding varying amounts of power depending upon the national importance of their god. One very influential figure was Taitai, high priest of Horus and "greatest of the five in the temple

of Thoth," "sole one in the heart of the king who has no failing." Other priests had specific roles: Tuthmosis was "head of the secrets in the chest of Anubis, *sem* priest in the good house and embalmer"; Nakht was an astronomer ("hour priest"), responsible for studying the stars and determining the propitious time for important rituals.

Women, too, served as members of the clergy—their role was mainly to entertain and energize the deities through music and dance. Tuya, the mother of Queen Tiy, was "singer of Amun," "singer of Hathor," "chief of the entertainers of Amun," and "chief of the entertainers of Min."

The temple workshops employed their own craftsmen, whose work lay at the heart of the country's religious life. "Chief stone sculptor" Men ultimately became "overseer of the works of the king" and was the architect responsible for creating the massive statues of Amenhotep that flanked the king's funerary temple—the so-called "colossi of Memnon."

A portrait of the vizier Ramose from his Theban tomb scenes. He is shown wearing the traditional dress of the vizier with several necklaces (including two *shebyu* collars) and holding a staff of office. Two priests are depicted ceremonially purifying the vizier.

Chapter Four

THE DAZZLING SUN

ca. 1371–1362BCE

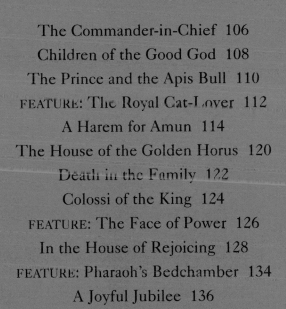

The face of Amenhotep III's recently discovered
red-quartzite statue represents the king in his deified
form after his first *sed* festival of regnal year 30.

THE COMMANDER-IN-CHIEF

YEAR 21 (ca. 1371BCE)

Amenhotep III maintained his country's status as the super-power of its era through the civilized art of diplomacy rather than by force. The troops who were no longer needed for military campaigns were redeployed to guard borders and to police the trade routes and mining areas that created Egypt's great wealth. Riches no longer diverted to fund foreign campaigns were used to pay for the king's building projects at home. But it would be a mistake to think that the Nubian campaign of ca. 1387BCE was the only military activity during Amenhotep's reign. The latest scholarly research is revealing that the king did not neglect his armed forces.

Amenhotep III seems to have been the first Egyptian king to employ chariotry as a separate section of the army: he used an élite chariot corps called the *maryannu* and appointed his father-in-law, Yuya, lieutenant-commander of chariotry. Horses were becoming more important in military engagements and the first Egyptian mounted soldiers were probably deployed around this time.

The king was the army's commander-in-chief. The pharaohs of the Eighteenth Dynasty did indeed lead their troops into battle and it seems likely that Amenhotep III himself fought in the campaign against Nubia. More usually, however, the king was represented in the field by his commanders. A reference to "King's son, troop commander Tuthmosis" on a whipstock found in Tutankhamun's tomb may refer to Amenhotep III's eldest son, Crown Prince Tuthmosis, or to a son of Tuthmosis IV.

A number of men who served in Amenhotep's armed forces had already proved themselves under the previous king. On Amenhotep's accession,

Nebamen continued in his post as "chief of the troops of police in western Thebes," while his brother Turi worked on the opposite bank of the river as "chief of the troops of police in (eastern) Thebes." A scribe of recruits, named Horemheb, served three kings in his career. "I followed the good god, lord of the two lands, Aakheperure [Amenhotep II], given life, his beloved son, lord of diadems, Menkheperure [Tuthmosis IV], given life, his beloved son, lord of the desert, Nebmaatra, son of Ra, Amenhotep, ruler of Thebes, beloved of Amun."

This detail of a painted relief scene from Hatshepsut's Deir el-Bahari funerary temple shows the military escort of a foreign trading expedition. The soldiers are typical of the mid-18th Dynasty in their dress and arms.

Soldiers known as "standard-bearers" served as commanders in charge of companies of between 200 and 250 infantry soldiers; each company was divided into platoons of 50 men, which were further divided into squads of 10 men. Larger divisions of up to 5,000 men were named in honor of the principal Egyptian deities, such as Amun and Ptah.

During peacetime the army was separated into two sections—one stationed in Memphis and one in Thebes—where men would be trained in both the arts of war and the use of weaponry. By the Eighteenth Dynasty the wide range of defensive and offensive equipment available included sickle-shaped *khepesh* swords, as depicted in portrayals of both the king and his troops. Daggers were also used, but the bow was a far more common weapon, expertly handled by men such as Wesi, "head of the bowmen of the lord of the Two Lands." Protective armor was worn from this period: scales of armor have been found at Amarna and an entire suit of leather body armor and eight shields formed part of the burial equipment of Tutankhamun.

Egypt also maintained a royal fleet, made up of ships with names such as "The Ruler is Strong" and "Star in Memphis." The fleet, which was headed by the king's own ship *Kha-em-maat*, meaning "Appearing in Truth," was led by the troop commander Nebenkemt of Sedment. Naval careers appear to have run in families: the "standard-bearer on the king's ship *Kha-em-maat*" was Siese, whose father Hatmesha had served as standard-bearer under King Tuthmosis IV on his ship *MeryAmun*, meaning "Beloved of Amun."

CHILDREN OF THE GOOD GOD

YEAR 22 (ca. 1370BCE)

After twenty years of marriage Amenhotep III and his great royal wife Tiy had produced a sizeable family. The eldest son, and heir to the throne, was Crown Prince Tuthmosis, named after his grandfather, Tuthmosis IV. Unlike most royal sons of this dynasty, who were rarely represented with their fathers, Tuthmosis was depicted with Amenhotep in an official capacity. Amenhotep gave his beloved son numerous titles and honors, associating him in particular with the northern capital of Memphis and its great temple of the god Ptah, where Tuthmosis —already a *sem* priest—was appointed high priest.

Sitamun, Amenhotep's daughter by Queen Tiy, is portrayed in this detail of a chair found in her grandparents' tomb (see also page 129).

As high priest of Ptah, Tuthmosis accompanied his father at the burial ceremony of the first Apis bull at Sakkara (see page 111). Tragically, Amenhotep was to preside at Tuthmosis's own burial ceremony, for the prince died before his father, who was ultimately succeeded by his second son, another Amenhotep (Amenhotep IV, later Akhenaten). The only certain reference to Prince Amenhotep from his father's reign appears to be on a jar seal inscribed "the estate of the king's son Amenhotep."

Reliefs and statuary often portray the king with his mother Mutemwia, his principal wife Tiy, and their daughters, four of whom are firmly identified as Sitamun (the eldest daughter), Henuttaneb, Isis, and Nebetah. Both Sitamun (in Year 30) and Isis (in Year 34) became their father's "great royal wife." Rather than literally indicating incest, this probably relates to the way in

which Amenhotep's favorite goddess, Hathor, was variously regarded as the mother, wife, or daughter of the sun god Ra. There is a fine portrait of Princess Sitamun on a gilded chair (see left) from the tomb of her grandparents, Yuya and Tuya. Inscribed "the daughter of the king, the great one, his beloved daughter Sitamun," it shows her enthroned receiving tribute of gold. The names of Sitamun, Henuttaneb, and Isis are also found on small decorative objects such as eyepaint containers and jewelry.

A princess called Beketaten appears as a tiny child with Amenhotep and Tiy in a relief in the tomb of Tiy's steward, Huy, at Amarna. Beketaten's exact parentage is uncertain, but she may have been the royal couple's youngest child. Another possible royal daughter, Iny, is known from a single canopic jar from a group burial of women of Amenhotep's court, while sixteen unnamed princesses described as "children of the king"—perhaps the offspring of minor wives—appear behind Tiy in the tomb of the royal steward Kheruef.

A limestone relief in the Theban tomb of Kheruef shows two unnamed "royal children" with sidelocks and small crowns shaking sistra (sacred rattles) as part of *sed* festival rites.

THE PRINCE AND THE APIS BULL

At Memphis, Egypt's traditional northern capital, the king founded a new temple dedicated to the creator god Ptah. It was named "Nebmaatra-united-with-Ptah" and embellished with a number of quartzite colossi of the god. Amenhotep later gave his eldest son, Crown Prince Tuthmosis, the prestigious role of high priest of Ptah, based at this important temple.

This painted statuette of a priest with an offering table may depict Amenhotep's son Tuthmosis, high priest of Ptah at Memphis.

Amenhotep gave responsibility for the construction of the Ptah temple to his steward of Memphis, Amenhotep Huy, making him "controller of works" and "overseer of works in the temple 'Nebmaatra-united-with-Ptah.'" A statue of Amenhotep Huy was erected within the new temple, close to the statue of the king himself. It bore an inscription describing how the steward made an endowment to the establishment, and how "his majesty praised me on account of my donations, and I appeared excellent in his heart." The inscription went on: "This statue was given to me by the king and placed in the house of 'Nebmaatra-united-with-Ptah.' His majesty gave me divine offerings that had come from before his statue in his temple and when the god had sated himself and this statue had received its meals, then the lector priest would take the offerings and they would be offered to this humble servant by the hand of the *waab* priest of the hour."

The temple personnel were appointed from the noble families of Memphis, with the priests—"servants of the god" or "prophets"—headed by the high priest as first prophet. In Memphis the high priest was known as the "greatest of controllers of craftsmen," because of Ptah's role as creator god and patron of

artisans, and held the title "overseer of the prophets of Upper and Lower Egypt." Ptah's high priest was distinguished by a sidelock attached to his short, round wig and a traditional jackal necklace. During Amenhotep's reign the office was held first by Ptahmose son of Tuthmosis, then by Ptahmose son of Menkheper, and ultimately by Crown Prince Tuthmosis, who had previously been a *sem* priest.

As high priest, Tuthmosis accompanied his father, the king, in the funeral ceremony of the first Apis bull to be buried at Sakkara. This event was portrayed in the relief scenes that decorated the original free-standing chapel built at the site by Amenhotep. The Apis bull was a sacred animal whose divine nature was indicated by a series of distinct white markings on an otherwise black hide. It was worshiped as the physical manifestation of Ptah, and was housed in a sanctuary near the god's temple at Memphis. On its death the bull became a form of Osiris, god of the afterlife, and the name "Osiris-Apis" was transformed in later times to that of the god Serapis. It is clear that the king wished to promote the ancient Apis cult that dated back to the very first dynasty of kings—an attitude that was not only in keeping with his enthusiastic support of traditional customs, but also highlighted his promotion of animal-based cults. Through association with lions, crocodiles, rams, and bulls he could emphasize many royal attributes—for example, the obvious strength of the bull was used as a standard symbol for the might of the king. Moreover, the Apis bull was the embodiment of Ptah and any royal support for the northern Memphite priesthood of Ptah effectively counterbalanced the power of Amun's clergy in the south.

Each bull was mummified in the traditional manner. To the accompaniment of great national mourning, it was borne in procession to the Memphite burial ground at Sakkara, where it was laid to rest in its own tomb. Here it was placed within a massive granite sarcophagus, complete with a set of huge canopic jars. The burial jars of the first Apis bull buried in Amenhotep III's reign had human-headed stoppers with the king's characteristic facial features; there were also pottery and alabaster jars bearing the name of Prince Tuthmosis.

The liver of the first Apis bull to be buried at the Serapeum was placed in this giant limestone canopic jar. The bull was buried at the Sakkara Serapeum during ceremonies led by the king and his son, High Priest Tuthmosis.

THE ROYAL CAT-LOVER

Amenhotep and his family had a great fondness for cats, a fact that is reflected in the animal's frequent appearance in art of the period. The royal couple's eldest son, Crown Prince Tuthmosis, was devoted to his pet cat, and it is ironic that the young man who buried the first Apis bull in a massive granite sarcophagus is now probably best known for the tiny limestone sarcophagus in which he laid his cat to rest.

Discovered in the vicinity of Memphis, the cat's sarcophagus is an important historical document since it gives the fullest surviving description of Tuthmosis's titles: "Crown Prince, overseer of the priests of Upper and Lower Egypt, high priest of Ptah in Memphis and *sem* priest." The prince's cat was called "Ta-Miu," "Lady Cat," her name containing the Egyptian word for cat, *miu*, which is simply the noise a cat makes, and quite similar to the name of the modern Egyptian breed Mau. Her name appears no fewer than eleven times on her sarcophagus, on which she is portrayed wearing an ornamental collar, seated on a cushion before an offering table on which rests a large duck. She is then shown in mummified form, and in the same way that humans' mummies were associated with Osiris after death, she is guarded by his sisters Isis and Nephthys. Prayers invoke the sky goddess Nut and the four sons of Horus are described as protecting her.

The religious symbolism of cats greatly influenced their appearance in tomb scenes. Their solar connection made them particularly appealing to Amenhotep since the cat was a representative of the sun god Ra. As the "Great Cat" he is referred to in Spell 17 in the Book of the Dead: "The Great Cat is the sun god himself"; he is shown in funerary scenes restoring order by decapitating the evil serpent Apophis—an allusion to wildcats' ferocity when tackling snakes. A similar symbolism can be seen in the image of the so-called "retriever cat" in the tomb paintings of the royal scribe Nebamun: the animal is shown helping to capture some wild fowl whose flapping wings symbolize disorder.

The cat was also associated with female divinity and prowess. As the domesticated form of the wild feline—the tamed Hathor to the wildness of Sekhmet—the cat was worshiped as the goddess Bastet. Her name, rendered phonetically using the hieroglyph of an alabaster perfume jar ("Bas"),

In a detail of a riverside hunting scene from the Theban tomb of the scribe Nebamun, the deceased's cat is shown catching waterfowl. The cat is shown helping to still the chaotic flapping of the wild birds, who symbolize disorder.

means "she of the perfume jar." While this may refer merely to the ritual purity involved in her cult, it is interesting to note that by tradition Bastet was the mother of Nefertem, young god of the lotus from which the sun rises, so she was literally the vessel that carried the lotus.

Perfume vessels were sometimes carved in feline form; one Middle Kingdom example took the shape of a wildcat and the feline motif was also used in a number of Eighteenth-Dynasty royal perfume jars. During New Year rituals the king protected himself from harm by anointing his body with the lotus perfumes of Nefertem, who was understood to be "protector of the Two Lands" and the son of the feline goddess Sekhmet.

A HAREM FOR AMUN

YEAR 25 (ca. 1367BCE)

In the middle years of his reign Amenhotep began building the temple "Southern Ipet," whose later Arabic title el-Aksur, "the castles," gave the modern town of Luxor its name. Set on the banks of the Nile, two miles (five kilometers) to the south of Karnak, the Luxor temple is the best preserved of all Amenhotep's Theban buildings. It was dedicated to Amun and referred to as the god's "southern harem" ("harem" literally means "private quarters"). The temple was the cult center of the divine royal *ka* or spirit, the place where the king renewed his powers through those of the god Amun during the annual Opet festival, which had been initiated by the female pharaoh Hatshepsut.

On a site considered to be sacred to the local god Amun since at least the Twelfth Dynasty, Queen Hatshepsut had built a small Opet shrine. Around this Amenhotep III erected a great temple. He rebuilt the shrine, renovated and extended the surrounding chambers into palatial quarters for the god, and built a solar court of perfectly proportioned lotus columns fronted by a colonnade hall that was 164 feet (50 meters) long. Recent scholarly examination of the building and its reliefs has shown that the solar court and colonnade hall were the last features to be built by the king, since the temple was actually constructed and decorated from the back to the front—beginning with the innermost shrines. The shrines include the birth chamber, decorated with scenes of Amenhotep's divine conception that were completed in time for his first *sed* or jubilee in the 30th year of his reign (see page 136).

Amenhotep also implemented Hatshepsut's plan to connect the Luxor and Karnak temples with a ceremonial way running north to south and lined with ram-headed sphinxes. In front of the Luxor temple itself he constructed a "viewing place," or *maru*, with a lake surrounded by gardens. The king described the lake and gardens on his funerary temple stela from Kom el-Hetan. "I made a viewing place facing Southern Ipet for my father Amun, a place of relaxation for him at his beautiful feast of Opet. It is planted with all kinds of flowers and Nun is happy in its lake. It has more wine than water, overflowing like Hapy at the inundation. An abode for the lord of eternity, it

THE FESTIVAL OF OPET

The Luxor temple, or "Southern Ipet," was built as a suitably beautiful place in which to celebrate the annual Opet (Ipet) festival, which took place during the second month of the yearly flood and lasted for between two and four weeks. Begun by the innovative Hatshepsut, the festival revived the pharaoh's powers through contact with the mighty god Amun.

During the festival Amun's cult statue, and those of his wife Mut and their son Khonsu, were all brought out from the Karnak sanctuary in sacred barques and either taken by river or carried in procession along the sphinx-lined route that linked Karnak and Luxor.

Worshipers believed that, in the inner sanctuary at the Luxor temple, Amun would ritually unite with the mother of the reigning monarch so that she could once again give birth to the royal *ku*. At the culmination of events the king entered the sanctuary, merged with his new-born *ka* in a secret ritual and then reappeared, as the son of Amun-Ra, replenished and vibrant with divine power.

Temple reliefs portray the stages of this great event. Those in Amenhotep's entry colonnade show the journey of the Theban triad as they traveled by river in their barques. Accompanied by great crowds, they were then received at the Luxor temple by a welcoming party of dancers, and great offerings of meat and bread were made. Once it had been presented and enjoyed by the gods, the food was redistributed to the waiting crowds.

The temple's dark inner sanctuary is decorated with depictions of the more mysterious rites, including the divine birth scenes, in which Amun united with the king's mother.

This detail of Ramesside reliefs at Luxor temple shows a fattened sacrificial bull being led by shaven-headed priests during an Opet festival procession.

is rich in offerings, receiving tribute from every foreign land, as numerous gifts are brought as tribute before Amun ... Silver, gold, cattle, all kinds of costly stones in their millions, hundred thousands, ten thousands, and thousands. I act for the one who begat me with affection, since he appointed me the Sun of the Nine Bows [the traditional enemies of Egypt], the king of Upper and Lower Egypt, Nebmaatra, the image of Ra, the son of Ra, Amenhotep, ruler of Thebes."

In addition to his new temple at Luxor, Amenhotep continued to beautify the Theban East Bank, embellishing the larger Karnak complex of Ipet-Sut by completing the third pylon, or monumental gateway, that then formed the temple's facade (see page 54). On its east face are inscriptions recording Amenhotep's reverent regard for Amun-Ra, with scenes showing the king making offerings to the god, to Amun's wife Mut, and to their son Khonsu, and depicting the divine triad's annual Opet festival procession. The king also added relief figures of himself to the west face of the fifth pylon and began work on a further pylon to face south. By the pylon's south face stood the greatest statue ever erected in Egypt: a massive quartzite figure of Amenhotep III (see page 124).

Amenhotep also set up a large granite scarab of Khepri (the sun god in the form of a scarab beetle) by the sacred lake and built a great temple granary

HEAVENLY MONUMENTS

Amenhotep's funerary temple stela records the king's own descriptions of his building works: "It pleased my heart to make very great monuments, the like of which had never existed since the beginning of the Two Lands." These include his Luxor and Karnak structures.

Of the Luxor temple he wrote: "The king of Upper and Lower Egypt, lord of the Two Lands, Nebmaatra, heir of Ra, son of Ra, lord of diadems, Amenhotep, ruler of Thebes, is happy with the work done in Southern Ipet for his father Amun, lord of the thrones of the Two Lands. It is made of fine sandstone, very wide and great and incredibly beautiful. Its walls are of fine gold, its pavements are of silver, and all its gates are worked with gold. Its pylons reach up into the sky and its flagpoles reach to the stars. When people see the temple they praise his majesty."

The inscription also describes the third pylon at Karnak. "The king made another monument for Amun, a very great gateway before Amun-Ra, lord of the thrones of the Two Lands, covered in gold throughout and carved with the god's image in the likeness of a ram, inlaid with real lapis-lazuli and worked with gold and costly stones. The like had never before been made. Its pavements are made of pure silver and its outer gate is set with stelae of lapis-lazuli on each side. Its two sides reach up to the sky like the four supports of heaven. Its flagpoles reach skyward and shine, worked in gold. His majesty brought the gold for it from the land of Karoy on his first campaign of victory of slaying vile Kush. The king of Upper and Lower Egypt, Nebmaatra, the beloved son of Amun-Ra, the son of Ra, Amenhotep, ruler of Thebes."

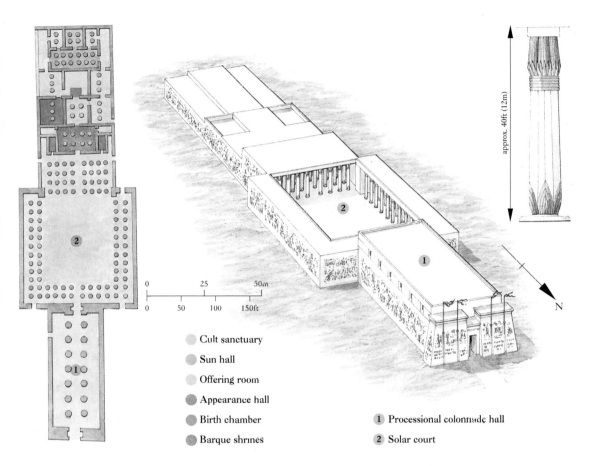

approx. 40ft (12m)

0   25   50m
0   50   100   150ft

- Cult sanctuary
- Sun hall
- Offering room
- Appearance hall
- Birth chamber
- Barque shrines

1 Processional colonnade hall
2 Solar court

N

in mudbrick faced with painted sandstone reliefs, to house the grain being produced by increasingly plentiful harvests (see pages 92–93).

On the periphery of Amun's complex the king built a small sandstone temple named "Khaemmaat." Although dedicated to Amun, its emphasis was solar—it included a Luxor-style solar court, a shrine to the sun god's daughter Maat, and two huge quartzite figures of the king adorned with abundant solar symbols. Amenhotep used vast amounts of precious materials to decorate his sacred structures and the recorded figures are breathtaking: more than 3 tonnes of electrum, 2.5 tonnes of gold, 924 pounds (420 kilograms) of copper, 1,250 pounds (560 kilograms) of lapis-lazuli, 215 pounds (97 kilograms) of turquoise, 1.5 tonnes of bronze, and 10 tonnes of copper.

The king also presented a votive clepsydra (water clock) to Karnak, with which the hour-priests could calculate the times for ritual proceedings in conjunction with their observation of the stars. The clepsydra bore figures of Amenhotep III making offerings to the sun god Ra and the moon god Thoth.

ABOVE LEFT
A plan of Luxor temple.
ABOVE CENTER
An artist's reconstruction of the temple as it is thought to have looked by the end of Amenhotep III's reign.
ABOVE RIGHT
An artist's reconstruction of one of the painted papyrus columns that lined the solar court.

OVERLEAF The temple of Luxor looking south from Amenhotep III's colonnade (right) toward his solar court (left).

THE HOUSE OF THE GOLDEN HORUS

YEAR 26 (ca. 1366BCE)

Amenhotep III's building activities were not confined to the great temples of Thebes. He sent his officials and craftsmen the length and breadth of the country to seek out sufficiently beautiful environments for the gods to inhabit, restoring old temples and creating magnificent new ones. Sometime during the third decade of his reign the king began the construction of a temple at Hebenu (Kom el-Ahmar, near Minya in Middle Egypt), close to the temple of Thoth at Hermopolis, where he also left his mark. Hebenu was one of the cult centers of Horus, and Amenhotep, as Horus's representative, described himself as "Nebmaatra, beloved of Horus, lord of Hebenu." Little remains of his original limestone structure, but a surviving part of its stunning, brightly painted raised-relief decoration suggests that a truly superb temple once stood on this site.

The king erected religious buildings right across Egypt, from the northern Delta to the Sudan. He honored Ra at Heliopolis, Ptah at Memphis, the Apis bull at Sakkara, Horus at Hebenu, Thoth at Hermopolis, Sobek at Sumenu, Khnum at Elephantine, and Nebmaatra—the king's divine self—at Soleb in Nubia. The god Amun-Ra was honored throughout the country.

Many of Amenhotep III's temples were built on old sites that were traditionally considered sacred. However, in founding a number of new temples on virgin land, he appears to have followed a deliberate plan to create an even distribution of important temples throughout the Nile Valley.

Part of the remaining wall decoration from Hebenu portrays four nome gods (divine figures representing Egypt's "nomes," or provinces) bringing their abundant produce to the king: great trays of bread, wheat, wildfowl, fish, fruit, flowers, eggs, and wine, with fattened sacrificial livestock following at their heels. Alternately colored red and blue, the nome deities are portrayed with the stocky and plump proportions that were developing as the reign progressed—the same proportions used at this time in representations of the king himself, to symbolize the wealth and abundance emanating directly from him.

The temple administration was headed by the high priest Taitai, who also worked at the nearby temple of Thoth. A highly polished grey-stone statuette of Taitai bears the inscription "hereditary noble and mayor, controller of the two thrones, overseer of priests, greatest of the five in the temple of Thoth, sole one in the heart of the king, with no failings, the high priest of Horus lord of Hebenu, Taitai." His body is carved in the same proportions as those found in contemporary reliefs.

Amenhotep honored other aspects of Horus at temples throughout Egypt. At Hebenu he was worshiped as the young warrior-god who vanquished Seth, the god of chaos. At Athribis in the Delta, the home town of the king's favorite official, Amenhotep son of Hapu, the pharaoh combined the solar aspect of Horus with the local god Khentikheti, and provided the god Horus-Khentikheti with a new temple in which Amenhotep Hapu's son served as high priest.

At the other end of his domains, in Nubia, Amenhotep III honored Horus with a temple at Aniba, while at Soleb he commissioned great black-granite statues of the god as a falcon, on which he is described as "beloved of Nekheny [Horus] who resides in Khaemmaat." Khaemmaat was the name of Amenhotep's Soleb temple and also one of the king's own titles, so this inscription effectively states that Horus resides in both the temple and the king himself. Indeed, the king was sometimes depicted wearing a feathered costume to identify him with Horus. The epithet "Nekheny" identifies Horus as "lord of Nekhen" (Hierakonpolis, a cult center of Horus) in southern Egypt, directly opposite Nekheb (el-Kab), the site of Amenhotep's early temple to the vulture goddess Nekhbet, and close to Horus's temple at Edfu, built much later.

A stone statuette of Taitai, high priest of Horus. He wears the panther skin and ornate apron of his office. His head is shaven as a mark of ritual purity.

DEATH IN THE FAMILY

YEAR 27 (ca. 1365BCE)

In the midst of a peaceful and prosperous reign, as the Two Lands flourished under Amenhotep's capable rule, the king's beloved eldest son Tuthmosis died. Not only was this a personal tragedy for Amenhotep, it was also a violent assault on the Egyptian world view: when son predeceased father, chaos had apparently replaced the natural order. The entire nation joined with the royal family to mourn the prince's death.

Prince Tuthmosis had been brought up to succeed his father and—named after his grandfather—had seemingly been destined to become Tuthmosis V in an alternating dynasty of kings named Tuthmosis or Amenhotep. Royal sons were rarely portrayed with their fathers during the Eighteenth Dynasty, yet Tuthmosis had been shown with his father in an official capacity, bearing the many titles and honors given to him in preparation for his future role.

In contrast to his elder brother, the royal couple's second son Amenhotep (who was named after his father but later changed his name to Akhenaten) had remained very much in the shadows. He is mentioned only on a jar inscription referring to "the estate of the king's son, Amenhotep," and while some scholars have suggested that father and son may have attempted rule by co-regency, this remains to be proven. The young prince must have been ill-prepared for the role that lay ahead of him. Indeed, his reign was to bring Egypt close to ruin.

Unfortunately the date and circumstances of Prince Tuthmosis's death are unknown: although his titles suggest that he spent much of his life at the northern capital Memphis, as the king's eldest son he was probably buried in Thebes. The unidentified mummy of a teenage boy was found reburied in the tomb of Prince Tuthmosis's great-grandfather Amenhotep II, lying between two female mummies. The royal resting place suggests that this is

a prince at the very least, and given the recent identification—through hair sampling—of the elder female mummy as possibly Queen Tiy, it is tempting to suggest that the boy is Tuthmosis himself, laid to rest with his mother.

As for the crown prince's original funeral equipment, a beautiful wooden coffin found in the Valley of the Queens displays the facial features associated with Amenhotep III's reign. Originally gilded, it was reused for the burial of a later prince—one of the sons of Ramesses III. In their superbly decorated tombs, Ramesses' sons appear with the father who outlived them, as he takes each one to meet the gods and ensures their safe passage into the afterlife. No doubt Prince Tuthmosis received the same care from his royal father.

Scenes from the Amarna Royal Tomb of Akhenaten give us an idea of how Eighteenth-Dynasty rulers mourned their dead. These scenes show the king and queen grief-stricken at the death of one of their children, throwing dirt over their heads in mourning as a reversal of normal practices of cleanliness. Another sign of grief was to let the hair become unkempt, pulling at it and allowing it to grow; a fascinating sketch on a limestone flake (ostracon) shows the head of a king in an attitude of mourning, with stubble on his unshaven and grief-contorted face.

This detail from the painted funeral scenes of the vizier Ramose shows his funerary equipment (a fan, sandals, perfume vessels, and *shabti* boxes) and furniture (a bed, a chair, and chests) being carried in procession to his grand Theban tomb. A similar, although more lavishly equipped, procession would have accompanied the funeral of Crown Prince Tuthmosis.

COLOSSI
OF THE KING

YEAR 28 (ca. 1364BCE)

As Amenhotep's reign progressed, the king's architects created ever-larger monuments to their master. In the twenty-eighth year of his rule, they erected a vast quartzite colossus of him—the largest statue ever built in Egypt. The monument—of which only the feet remain today (see below, right)—rose 70 feet (21 meters) above the south side of the tenth pylon at Karnak.

The red-quartzite figure of Amenhotep III recently discovered in a cache beneath the floor of Luxor temple portrays the king in his fully deified state as the "dazzling Aten" and is 8.1ft (almost 2.5m) tall.

The king's official, Amenhotep son of Hapu, left an awe-inspiring description of this magnificent statue: "great in size, its beauty surpasses that of the pylon. It is ... set up in his great house [Karnak] to endure like heaven." The size of the statue's feet, which measure 10 feet (3 meters) in length, gives an idea of the grandeur of the figure. In his capacity as "overseer of all the king's works," Amenhotep son of Hapu obtained the quartzite used for the statue from the quarries of Gebel Ahmar around 420 miles (700 kilometers) to the north, near modern Cairo. An inscription reports, "I created for his majesty a mountain of quartzite."

There are more than 1,000 surviving monumental statues of Amenhotep as king or god, more than 45 of which are more than 10 feet (3 meters) high. Many figures are still in good condition, and none more so than the cache of statues found beneath the solar court of the Luxor temple. This cache includes statues of both the king and various gods and goddesses.

The most magnificent of the group, and possibly the most magnificent of all Egyptian statues, is a red-quartzite figure of the king in almost pristine condition (illustrated opposite). He appears in the double crown of the united Egypt with the wide uraeus-serpent collar and a jeweled apron (set with uraei and topped with solar disks) over a finely pleated kilt with a feather detail. He has sandals on his feet and stands on a sledge, a deified pose normally associated with deceased kings, but used for Amenhotep because he became immortal, a living god imbued with the powers of the sun, at around the time of his first *sed*, or jubilee festival, in the 30th year of his reign. Inscriptions sing his praises: that on the back pillar hails him as "the true king ... the one great in sacred and splendid monuments."

Across the Nile from Luxor, Amenhotep's Kom el-Hetan funerary temple on the Theban West Bank was adorned with a series of 25-foot (8 meter) figures of the king as Osiris, the god of the afterlife. Erected between the columns of the temple's great solar court, the granite figures on the south side of the court wore the white crown of Upper Egypt, while the quartzite statues on the north side wore the red crown of Lower Egypt.

Today only the feet of the quartzite colossus of Amenhotep III survive. Bearing the name "Nebmaatra, Montu of Rulers" (Montu was the Theban war god), the statue stood beside the tenth pylon at Karnak temple.

THE FACE OF POWER

A menhotep's subjects believed that images of their king were imbued with divine essence. Royal statues became objects of worship in themselves: they were given their own names and set up in the ruler's many temples. Their great size and beauty inspired awe in the illiterate majority, while the finely carved inscriptions impressed the literate élite.

According to a stela found in his funerary temple at Kom el-Hetan, the face of Amenhotep shone "down on the faces of the people like Aten when he shines at dawn." Statues of Egyptian monarchs are distinguishable by their facial features. The characteristic traits of Amenhotep's face are the large almond-shaped eyes, which combine with a small retroussé nose and smiling lips to produce a somewhat androgynous effect. The extent of the cosmetic lines on the eyes provides scholars with a means of dating the figures within the reign (see opposite). As for Queen Tiy, her features tended to follow those of the king, although her slightly pouting lips often turn downward a little.

Among the individuals responsible for creating the royal image were the twin brothers Suti and Hor, both architects, who held the title "overseer of the works of Amun" at Karnak and Luxor respectively. Other royal artisans include Huy, who described himself as a "sculptor of Amun," Ipuki the "pharaoh's sculptor," and Nebamun the "pharaoh's head sculptor." Ipuki and Nebamun were evidently close colleagues—they chose to be buried together in a tomb with exquisitely detailed scenes that show the kinds of work they contributed to the reign's magnificent artistic legacy. Such skilled craftsmen worked in a variety of stone, from the king's favorite black granite to brown quartzite, white limestone, and creamy alabaster (calcite). Small-scale figurines were generally made of limestone, calcite, steatite, wood, glazed faience ware, or even solid gold.

Many later kings used Amenhotep's huge funerary temple as a source of ready-made statuary. Ramesses II removed six of Amenhotep's granite figures while adding to Luxor temple, and even had his predecessor's distinctive facial features replaced with his own—at least one of the seated colossi in the Ramesseum, Ramesses' funerary temple, was recarved in this way. Near by,

LEFT A red-granite head of Amenhotep III wearing the crown of Upper Egypt, from his funerary temple at Kom el-Hetan.

EYES OF THE KING

The statues of Amenhotep III can often be dated from the way in which his sculptors carved the eyes, as the style varied over the course of his reign (see below). The heavy lines extending from the eyes and eyebrows (1 and 2) were often reduced later in the reign to simple outlines of the eyes (4). The fold sometimes added to the upper eyelid (3) may indicate the king's advancing age.

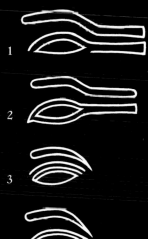

the fallen granite colossus that inspired Shelley's poem *Ozymandias*—the ancient Greek name for Ramesses II, derived from his throne-name Usermaatra —is thought to be of Amenhotep III, rather than Ramesses. Merneptah, the son of Ramesses II, also usurped Amenhotep's statues, but he simply engraved his cartouche on them rather than remodeling the faces. Larger limestone figures of Amenhotep with the gods were moved to Merneptah's Qurna funerary temple, which was itself largely made up of blocks reused from Amenhotep's buildings.

IN THE HOUSE OF REJOICING

YEAR 29 (ca. 1363BCE)

Designed to be attached to a chest containing written texts, this small faience bookplate bears the name of the king, "the good god, Nebmaatra, given life, loved by Amun-Ra, lord of the heavens, and ruler of Thebes." The king may have had his own library at Malkata.

At the end of his third decade as king, Amenhotep moved his court permanently to Thebes, where he had built "the palace of the dazzling Aten." Later known by its Arabic name, Malkata, "the place where things are picked up" (because it is littered with ancient debris), the palace stood on the Theban West Bank below the western hills where the sun set each evening, and directly opposite the king's temple of Luxor. Amenhotep's move to Thebes was in direct contrast with the behavior of previous pharaohs, who had based themselves at the traditional capital of Memphis and had only come south to Thebes for the annual religious festivals, setting up temporary court in palace buildings attached to Karnak temple. In constructing an independent palace, not only at the other end of the city from Karnak, but also on the opposite bank of the river, Amenhotep was clearly distancing himself from the Karnak clergy.

Amenhotep's Malkata palace was discovered by archaeologists in 1888, and subsequent excavations have revealed a site sprawling over 30 hectares, which was still being added to and embellished at the time of the king's death. The main areas of the palace that Amenhotep liked to call his "House of Rejoicing" were the king's own apartments in the southeast section, Queen Tiy's apartments to the south, those of their daughter Sitamun to the north, quarters for the rest of the royal family and numerous royal women, and residences for high officials and servants. There were also the administrative areas of the "west villas" and royal workshops, with a workers' village to the south. To the north lay a large settlement that acted as a support town to the palace; past it ran the causeway that linked Malkata to the king's funerary temple almost a mile (1.5 kilometers) away. The causeway also extended southeast into the desert to the nearby Kom el-Samak, the site of a brightly painted mudbrick platform built for the king's *sed* jubilee festivals (see pages 136–139).

To the north of the palace was a separate temple of Amun with a large court and a processional way linking it to a T-shaped harbor named Birket Habu. The harbor, 1.5 miles (2.5 kilometers) wide, fronted the palace and linked the royal residence to the Nile, providing access for both commercial and administrative traffic, as well as mooring space for the great golden barge *The Dazzling Aten*, on which the royal couple appeared during festivals.

Workmen built the Malkata palace complex using largely standard mud-bricks stamped with the king's names, although the bricks used for Tiy's

FURNISHINGS FOR A ROYAL HOUSE

Living close to the palace in their own village to the south, the royal craftsmen worked directly under the king's instructions and were supervised by "the great chamberlain in the great house," also named Amenhotep. They produced a dazzling array of furniture and household items intended for both home consumption and export abroad; items from the royal workshops at Malkata have been found as far afield as Babylon and Mycenae.

The cosmopolitan sophistication of the goods produced is indicative of the free flow of gifts and ideas between the monarchs of the ancient world. In a letter to Kadashman-Enlil, King of Babylon, Amenhotep listed the magnificent gifts he was sending: "a bed of ebony overlaid with ivory and gold; three beds of ebony overlaid with gold; one large chair of ebony overlaid with gold; nine chairs of ebony overlaid with gold. The weight of the gold on all these things is seven minas, nine shekels, and the weight of the silver one mina, eight and a half shekels." The Egyptian king also sent "ten footrests of ebony, overlaid with gold."

Small-scale artifacts in wood, stone, metal, ivory, glass, and faience produced at Malkata testify to the remarkable skill of the craftsmen there. Egyptian faience ware was manufactured in a range of colors at this time, from various shades of blue, turquoise, and purple to red, green, yellow, and white. Recent research has shown that the king's favorite color of faience was cobalt blue and has revealed that almost 70 per cent of the surviving colored glassware from Malkata is also in this shade.

The oldest known Egyptian glass factory was situated in the palace complex. It produced delicate perfume bottles and kohl tubes, mostly in cobalt blue.

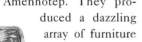

The gilded wooden chair of Sitamun, Amenhotep's eldest daughter, was found in her maternal grandparents' tomb.

These fragments of painted plaster from the palace at Malkata are decorated with naturalistic scenes depicting papyrus groves filled with wild geese, bordered by a frieze of rosettes.

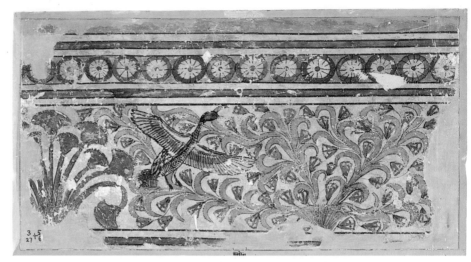

apartments were also stamped with her name. The walls were then plastered and the exteriors painted white. The workmen fitted door and window frames in more durable materials such as wood, limestone, and sandstone; they used wood for shelving and stone for column bases, steps, drainage systems, and bathrooms. The general level of luxury in the palace is indicated by the presence of bathroom facilities and well-tended, walled gardens with pools.

The rooms of the palace were painted in vivid colors, and from the thousands of fragments of painted plaster littering the site it is possible to reconstruct much of the original décor. It featured naturalistic scenes of animals and plants, interspersed with figures of the gods and amuletic devices, all

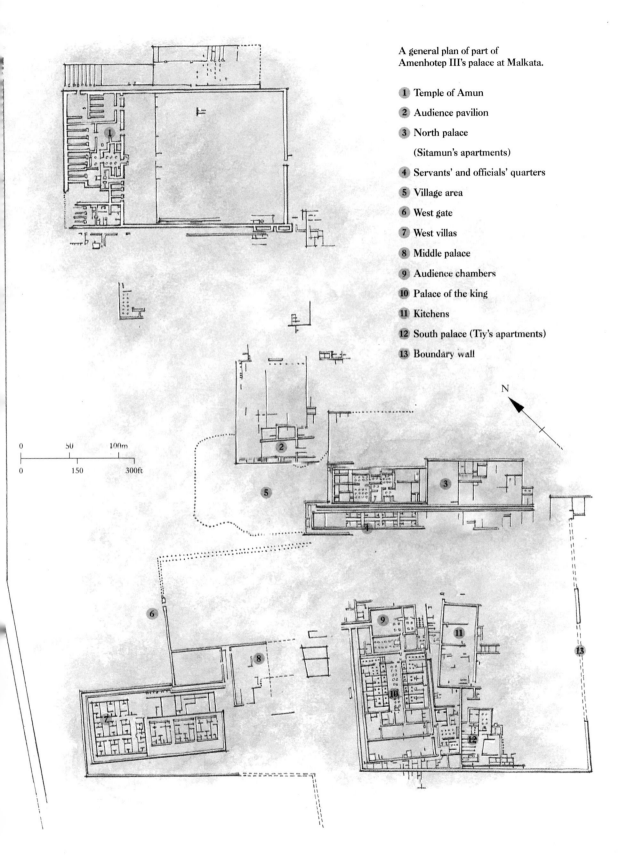

A general plan of part of
Amenhotep III's palace at Malkata.

1 Temple of Amun

2 Audience pavilion

3 North palace

   (Sitamun's apartments)

4 Servants' and officials' quarters

5 Village area

6 West gate

7 West villas

8 Middle palace

9 Audience chambers

10 Palace of the king

11 Kitchens

12 South palace (Tiy's apartments)

13 Boundary wall

N

0   50   100m

0   150   300ft

ROYAL SERVANTS

Vizier Amenhotep Huy and Chancellor Ptahmose worked closely with the king on a daily basis and resided near to his quarters in the palace. The vizier met every day with the royal seal-bearer, who was responsible for the contents of the storerooms and treasury. Vizier, chancellor, and seal-bearer all regularly consulted the royal stewards: Amenemhat Surero, the Theban steward; Meriptah, the steward of the king's funerary temple; and Nefersekheru, the steward of the Malkata palace itself.

All the members of the royal family had their own stewards in charge of their separate households within the palace. Kheruef ("Senaa") was Tiy's Malkata steward, while the now-elderly official Amenhotep son of Hapu acted as steward to the king's daughter Sitamun. Userhet was overseer of the royal apartments.

Constantly attended by fan-bearers "on the king's right-hand," Amenhotep was also served by a butler, a royal cup-bearer (who was responsible for His Majesty's comfort), and a master vintner.

Male and female musicians and dancers—women such as the royal mother-in-law Tuya, "singer of Amun and Hathor"—were as important a feature at court as they were in temple daily life. The task of providing diversions for the king was almost compar-able to that of entertaining the gods. Evocative images from the later Eighteenth-Dynasty Amarna tombs portray Egyptian and Syrian women in the palace harem

A scene from the joint Theban tomb of the sculptors Nebamun and Ipuki shows craftsmen in the royal workshop.

quarters dancing, singing, and playing harps, lyres, and lutes.

Skilled craftsmen populated the palace workshops—artists such as Nebamun and Ipuki, both of whom were employed by the king as royal sculptors, and Men, the "chief stone sculptor."

Various tomb and temple representations of the time cap-ture for posterity the figures of domestic servants busy around the palace, preparing and carry-ing food, sweeping the floors, and sprinkling water to keep down the dust. Some of the ser-vants' everyday tools have been found at the Malkata site, from kitchen knives, fish hooks, and chisels to a fiber paintbrush still covered in red paint.

enhanced with gilded and glazed tiles and inlays. The high-ceilinged audience chambers, one of which was 100 feet (30 meters) long, had tiled and painted floors featuring a repeated series of bound captives who were symbolically trampled underfoot by anyone crossing the floor. The red, blue, and yellow ceiling of the connecting royal robing room was decorated with a series of S-spirals and stylized bulls' heads, while leaping red and white calves, birds in flight, and lush floral motifs adorned the nearby "harem" (the private suites of the king's close family and royal women, which flanked the columned hall preceding the throne room). A naturalistic motif was also used on the floors of the hall, which were painted to represent the Nile, its waters teeming with fish and birds flying gracefully out from its verdant banks.

The colorful interiors of the palace would have been further enhanced by superbly crafted furniture and ornaments, at the very least comparable with the pieces found in the tomb of Tutankhamun: beds inlaid with ebony and gold, with lion-paw feet and linen sheets; gilded and inlaid chairs; cross-legged wooden stools painted to look like animal hide; large feather-stuffed cushions; fringed wallhangings; jewel caskets, wigboxes, and cosmetic chests; game boards; candlesticks; flower vases; gold and silver tableware; and vessels of alabaster, glass, faience, and pottery. Much of the pottery produced in Amenhotep's Malkata workshops was equally superb, its graceful forms painted or molded with plant and animal motifs, or with female figures and images of Hathor, goddess of beauty and joy, or the fertility god Bes.

Some of the palace rooms had built-in, wood-topped shelves for the storage of smaller portable items, although most possessions were stored in chests or caskets. The variety of small personal items found at the site helps to bring its inhabitants back to life: during their excavations archaeologists have uncovered rings, bracelets, necklaces, amulets, cosmetic spoons, kohl tubes, mirror handles, tweezers, and perfume bottles.

Small faience bookplates dating from the reign and bearing the names of the king and queen may indicate that the king had his own library at Malkata—a *per medjat* ("house of books") like those found in contemporary temples. These labels suggest that Amenhotep was interested in horticulture: one is inscribed "the book of the moringa tree" and another, "the book of the pomegranate tree." Archaeologists have also discovered writing equipment and scarab seals, and in one of the administrative "west villas" they have found hundreds of clay seals from rolls of official papyri.

PHARAOH'S BEDCHAMBER

At the heart of Amenhotep's new royal palace were his own private rooms, of which the most important was the royal bedchamber. This was 25 feet (8.3 meters) long and 15 feet (5 meters) wide, except at one end, which was slightly narrower and on a higher level than the rest of the room. It was in this raised alcove that Amenhotep slept, under fine linen sheets, on an elegant and skillfully crafted wooden bedstead, similar to others that have survived from this reign. Pairs of figures of the fertility god Bes adorned the west wall.

Assassination attempts on sleeping pharaohs were not unknown, so Amenhotep went to great lengths to ensure his safety at night. His head rested on a wooden neckrest—rather than pillows, Egyptians used "props" covered in fabric—decorated with magical protective symbols. The walls of his bedchamber were the thickest in the palace and were adorned with the repeated hieroglyphs *ankh* (☥, "life") and *sa* (𓍘, "protection").

VISITORS TO THE ROYAL APARTMENTS

Amenhotep would begin the day's business in the royal bedchamber and in its adjoining bathroom and dressing room. As pharaohs were divine, Amenhotep's every action was that of a god, including the act of getting up in the morning. His personal chambers were the setting for special daily ceremonies known as "the Ritual of the House of the Morning," which accompanied his rising, washing, and dressing. Assisting the king in these rites were royal officials and his personal servants, especially his butler Neferronpet, "the Pure of Hands"—a fitting name for one

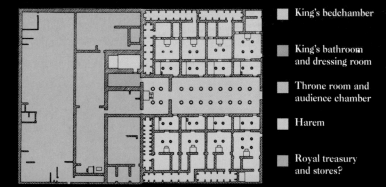

■ King's bedchamber

■ King's bathroom and dressing room

■ Throne room and audience chamber

■ Harem

■ Royal treasury and stores?

who was doubtless among the very few servants allowed to have physical contact with the king.

After the morning ritual Amenhotep received the first visitors of the day. These might be family, such as Queen Tiy—who had her own apartments in the South Palace—and the royal

children. Moving on to official matters, the king would then exchange daily reports with his "inner cabinet," consisting of the two highest ministers in the royal administration—the viceroys of Upper and Lower Egypt—together with the chancellor and the finance minister.

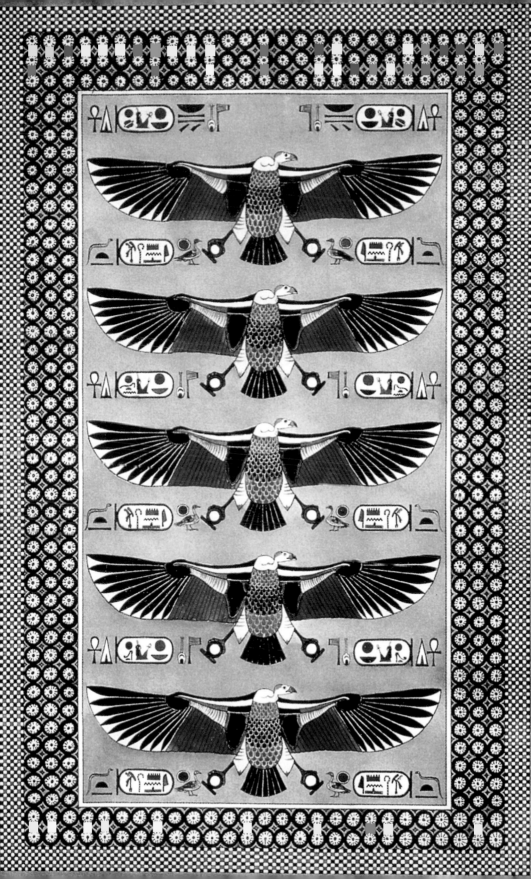

A JOYFUL JUBILEE

YEAR 30 (ca. 1362BCE)

In May of the thirtieth year of his reign Amenhotep held the first of his three great *sed*, or jubilee, festivals. At festivities in the specially built hall at Malkata, he declared himself Egypt's living god, the sun god's image on earth; he was already worshiped in the south of the country as the lunar god Nebmaatra, lord of Nubia. As part of the *sed* Amenhotep elevated his daughter Sitamun to the rank of "great royal wife."

The *sed* festival of renewal and regeneration was designed to reinvigorate the king—by infusing him anew with divine power—and so reconfirm his right to reign after 30 years of rule. Having proved himself through various *sed* rituals, the pharaoh would be acclaimed again as king of Upper and Lower Egypt and would receive the homage of his people. The earliest evidence for the *sed* dates to the First-Dynasty reign of King Den in the early third millennium BCE. King Djoser's Third-Dynasty Step Pyramid complex at Sakkara is the earliest surviving architectural setting for the ceremonies and later Fifth-Dynasty reliefs show Niusserre celebrating the rituals. Inspired by the elaborate *sed* festivals of the Middle Kingdom (ca. 2040–1640BCE), Amenhotep resolved to hold his own *sed* on a grand scale, as the pharaohs of the distant past had done before him.

The *sed* rites involved the king proving his physical prowess: ritual tests included running between two sets of boundary markers representing Egypt's borders in order to establish his claims on the land, and raising the great *djed* pillar that was a symbol of stability and stood for the backbone of Osiris. Once such tasks had been accomplished, the king received the regalia and emblems of both Upper and Lower Egypt, symbolizing his rule over a united land. During the rituals the monarch wore knee-length *sed* robes, including a traditional, tightly wrapped jubilee cloak decorated with diamond patterns.

Judging from the sheer number of inscribed containers found at the Malkata site, the provision of meat, fruit, honey, beer, and wine at the *sed* festival was lavish. The best wines were imported from Syria and events were presided over by Hathor—the goddess hailed as the "lady of drunkenness"—to the accompaniment of dancing, singing, and revelry. The proceedings involved the participation of the royal women, courtiers, and officials at every level. Men proud to have taken part in the *sed* often referred to their roles—and rewards—in their funerary inscriptions. Generous gifts given out during the celebrations included gold *shebyu* collars and items inscribed with the royal names.

The main player in the *sed* events was Amenhotep son of Hapu, the "festival leader" and "hereditary prince in the offices of the *sed* festival," who received numerous honors at the end of the celebration. As a reward for having presented the king with the records of a timely series of bumper harvests, Khaemhat, the overseer of granaries, was awarded the "gold of honor"; he also served as "priest of Anubis on the jubilee day of his majesty's first *sed* festival." Nebmerutef officiated as chief lector priest and the king's brother-in-law, the priest Anen, was no doubt in close attendance.

Queen Tiy's steward Kheruef, the individual responsible for organizing *sed* festivities at Malkata, also received a golden *shebyu*, while Nefersekheru acted as "custodian of the boundary markers in the broad hall," the route along which the king had to run—just as his predecessor Den had done more than 1,500 years earlier. Nefersekheru served as "controller of the double throne in the jubilee" in conjunction with the high priest Taitai and Viceroy Merymose, who had traveled north from Nubia. Even the northern governor Khaemwaset came south to take part in the festival.

Tantalizing glimpses of Amenhotep's *sed* festivities are found in several temple and tomb decorations from the reign: the most complete are those in the tomb of Kheruef, but representations of the *sed* also survive in the tomb of Khaemhat and the funerary temples of both the king and Amenhotep son of Hapu. The *sed* events are described in the inscription in Kheruef's tomb. "Rewards were given consisting of gold of honor, gold figurines of fish and ducks, and ribbons of

A statuette of the royal scribe and seal-bearer Nebmerutef, who officiated at Amenhotep's *sed*, shows him seated at work beneath the gaze of the moon god Thoth, who was the patron deity of scribes.

This relief figure of Khaemhat, the overseer of the granaries, is from his Theban tomb. The official is depicted wearing an intricately styled double wig, a collar, and a beaded necklace with a heart-shaped pendant.

green linen. All present were made to stand in order of rank. All were fed a royal breakfast of bread, beer, beef, and fowl. They were then directed to his majesty's lake, where they rowed the king's barque, grasping the tow rope of the evening barque and tow rope of the morning barque, and all towed the barques to the great place, stopping at the steps of the throne."

Amenhotep son of Hapu was then able to declare, "Amenhotep, ruler of Thebes, he is Ra, to whom is given an eternity of *sed* festivals." Having ritually proven his right to rule, before being borne across the waters in his golden barque, Amenhotep III had "died" as a mortal king to be infused with the goddess Hathor's vitality and then reborn as a god, eternally youthful, the dazzling *Aten*, the sun disk of all lands.

Kheruef's tomb scenes emphasize the vital role played by the royal women at the *sed* festival. In superbly cut reliefs, the king, dressed in his *sed* costume, sits enthroned in the embrace of Hathor, while Tiy stands behind them in full regalia, "in the following of the king, like Maat in the following of Ra," according to the inscription. As the sun god, Amenhotep is surrounded by the combined power of three generations of royal consorts: his mother Mutemwia, his wife Tiy, and Sitamun, his eldest daughter and new great royal wife. The group symbolizes Hathor's triple role as the mother, the wife, and the daughter of Ra.

The reliefs also show male musicians and dancers performing before the assembled royal family, the gyrations of acrobatic dancers leading to the climax of the rituals. An accompanying song asks the goddess to take the king safely to the horizon, where he can be reborn anew. "O sing to Hathor the Golden One, sweet pleasures for the Lady of the Two Lands so she may make Nebmaatra endure ... O Hathor, exalted by Ra, to you has been given the sky, the night, and the stars ... Protect Nebmaatra, give him life. Make him healthy in the east of the sky, so he is happy, prosperous, and healthy in the horizon. If you desire he should live, cause him to live for millions of years without end!"

The figure of Queen Tiy is followed by a row of 16 unnamed princesses described as "children of the king." Although some of them may have been the daughters of Amenhotep's minor wives, scholars believe that others were the children of foreign monarchs who had come to pay homage to the deified pharaoh. Foreign rulers were certainly invited to *sed* festivals. When the honor of an invitation was not extended, the slight was keenly felt; the Babylonian king Kadashman-Enlil I wrote to Amenhotep to complain bitterly that he had not received an invitation to the *sed*, adding an invitation to his own palace festivities in order to score points against his fellow monarch: "when you celebrated your great festival, you did not send your messenger to me saying, 'Come to eat and drink' ... I have built a new house, which your messengers have seen, and they are pleased with it. I am going to have a house-warming. Come yourself and eat and drink with me, I shall not act as you yourself did!"

REVIVING THE PAST

According to an inscription in the tomb of Kheruef, "generations of men since the time of the ancestors had not celebrated *sed*-festival rites, but it was commanded for Amenhotep, son of Amun ... his majesty did this in accordance with the ancient writings." In reviving the *sed* festival Amenhotep recreated ancient ceremonies not seen on such a scale in Egypt since the pyramid age.

The pharaoh researched the traditional festivities with great care. While his leading official, Amenhotep son of Hapu, (see pages 98–99) checked temple archives, other royal scribes were sent out to visit the ancient sites and report back on the reliefs and inscriptions they saw there. The Old Kingdom's northern pyramid sites were to prove inspirational.

At Sakkara the *sed*-festival courts of Djoser were highly informative. One of the royal scribes recorded his research trip to Meidum: "Regnal year 30 ... the scribe May came to view this very great pyramid of the Horus Snofru."

Amenhotep ordered that many of the ancient sites be restored to their former glory. In one inscription at Karnak the pharaoh boasts that, in places where existing monuments were enlarged or enhanced, "I made buildings anew, without damaging what had been done before." Amenhotep appears to have been particularly impressed by the acheivements of his predecessor Hatshepsut; he admired her planned causeway linking Luxor to Karnak, where relief scenes commemorated her own *sed* festival, and was inspired by her divine birth scenes, as well as her Opet festival rituals.

A range of family heirlooms, including several objects naming Hatshepsut and Tuthmosis III, have been found at the site of Amenhotep's Malkata palace (see pages 128–133).

Chapter Five

THE ROAD TO ETERNITY

ca. 1361–1354BCE

Grief-stricken female mourners are depicted in this
detail of a wallpainting from the tomb of Ramose,
one of Amenhotep's most prominent officials.

AN EVERLASTING MONUMENT

YEAR 31 (ca. 1361BCE)

Work was now well underway on Amenhotep III's funerary temple at Kom el-Hetan on the West Bank, close to his Malkata palace and the Theban cliffs where his rock-cut tomb lay. Designed to perpetuate the king's name and sustain his soul for ever, the temple was the greatest ever built in Egypt—scholars recently made the astonishing calculation that it was once even larger than Karnak.

This colossal quartzite head of Amenhotep III wearing the red crown of Lower Egypt was found on the north side of the great solar court of the Kom el-Hetan funerary temple.

Amenhotep planned his temple on a vast scale as a place of innovation: its sandstone walls, gleaming with gold, were adorned with relief scenes similar to those visible today at the Luxor and Soleb temples. The king, his family, and courtiers were shown celebrating his jubilee festivals in the company of the gods of Egypt, all of whom were present in the temple in sculpted form. Unfortunately, repeated plundering and ancient earthquake damage has left little of this great construction visible today.

Colossal figures, representing the king seated or striding forward, adorned the temple. The celebrated "Colossi of Memnon"—originally "ruler of rulers" but renamed by Greek visitors after the legendary king of Ethiopia who was killed by Achilles at Troy—still stand to mark the temple's eastern entrance pylon. The colossi feature the king in the company of three generations of royal wives, Mutemwia, Tiy, and one of his daughters (probably Sitamun).

At the temple's south gateway stood the largest dyad, or paired statue, ever carved: more than 23 feet (7 meters) tall, it represented Amenhotep seated with Tiy and their three daughters at their feet—Henuttaneb in the center, Nebetah on the right, and their unnamed sister, possibly Isis, on the left. A series of 26-foot (8-meter) figures of the king as Osiris, lord of the

West and god of the afterlife, stood between the great columns of the temple's central solar court, which was wide open to the sun. Its column bases and fragments of the original sculptures remain in situ today.

Near Kom el-Hetan, Amenhotep also constructed a special landing stage to welcome Amun's statue when, as part of the annual Beautiful Festival of the Valley, it was transported from Karnak to the West Bank. There the statue was taken to visit the funerary temples of the dead kings and infuse them with new life.

Given the low-lying ground chosen for the Kom el-Hetan temple, parts would have been submerged during the annual flood. This must have been intentional: as the floods receded, the temple and its statuary would have risen up in a symbolic act of rebirth, as if from the waters of creation. The temple was well supplied with offerings; one inscription stated, "its storerooms hold wealth beyond measure ... ." Such offerings would have been made by the temple's priests, who maintained the cult of the king and were active at least into Ramesside times, a century after Amenhotep's death.

One of the few remains at Kom el-Hetan is this stela, one of two that flanked the entrance to the solar court.

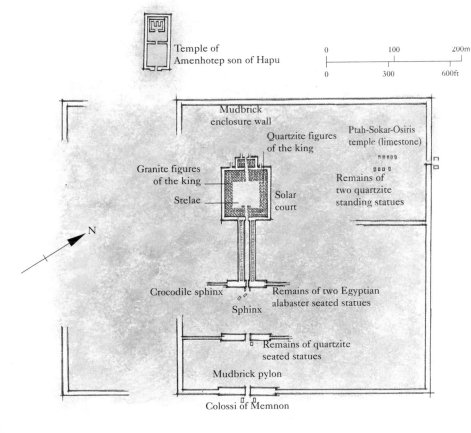

Temple of Amenhotep son of Hapu

| 0 | 100 | 200m |
| 0 | 300 | 600ft |

Mudbrick enclosure wall

Quartzite figures of the king

Ptah-Sokar-Osiris temple (limestone)

Granite figures of the king

Remains of two quartzite standing statues

Stelae

Solar court

N

Crocodile sphinx

Remains of two Egyptian alabaster seated statues

Sphinx

Remains of quartzite seated statues

Mudbrick pylon

Colossi of Memnon

A plan of the funerary temple of Amenhotep III at Kom el-Hetan showing the extent of the original enclosure walls and the three pylons leading to the great solar court.

DAYS OF MOURNING

YEAR 32 (ca. 1360BCE)

In the last decade of Amenhotep's reign the king buried his mother, Mutemwia, mourning the person who, in her role as regent, had guided him through a maze of protocol after the death of Tuthmosis IV. Queen Tiy's brother Anen had also died, shortly after the *sed* jubilee festival of ca. 1362BCE, and in this period Amenhotep's thoughts must have turned to his own mortality. Labels on wine jars in the storeroom of the king's great tomb in the West Valley indicate that perishable commodities were already being stored there in readiness for Amenhotep's own long journey into eternity.

The mummy of Yuya, Amenhotep's father-in-law, is the most perfectly preserved Egyptian mummy. It retains its eyelashes, eyebrows, stubbly chin, and even its blond hair.

The "great royal wife, god's mother" Mutemwia was at least 50 years old at the time of her death, so the king had been granted plenty of time in which to prepare a splendid tomb for her. It was most probably located in the Theban hills of Qurna—possibly in the Valley of the Queens, which lies just northwest of Malkata and is a smaller version of the Valley of the Kings. At the head of the Valley of the Queens is a great chasm that was held to be sacred to the cow goddess from predynastic times, and which came to be identified with the womb of Hathor in her capacity as Lady of the West residing in the Theban hills—the womb from which the dead are reborn each morning. It was an eminently suitable location in which to inter the mother of the king and to build the tombs of Amenhotep's sisters Tiaa and Amenemipet, who also died during his reign.

The location of Tiaa's and Amenemipet's original tombs is unknown, but a reburial of a group of queens, princesses, and noblewomen was discovered in a rock-cut tomb at the foot of the Qurna mountains, where they had been reinterred sometime during the Twenty-First Dynasty. The women's canopic jars mentioned Malkata and their damaged mummies bore wooden labels, that of Amenhotep's sister Princess Tiaa naming her "King's daughter of Menkheperure [Tuthmosis IV] of the House of the Royal Children." The decor of the women's original tombs must have been superb, to judge from the sumptuous colors and sophisticated, elegant styles found in the contemporary tombs of royal relatives and courtiers. Similarly, the contents of the original tombs must have been at least equal in magnificence to the splendid artifacts Amenhotep that provided for the burial of Queen Tiy's mother and father.

Tiy's parents, Yuya and Tuya, had probably died earlier in the reign. Their small tomb, located in the royal burial ground in the Valley of the Kings, was discovered largely intact, with bouquets of flowers laid out in the entrance passage. It was filled with superb objects of practical use: wooden beds overlaid with gold and silver and set with Bes figures; three gilded chairs decorated with figures of Yuya's and Tuya's granddaughter Sitamun; a turquoise faience and gold casket, set with the names of their daughter and royal son-in-law; a chariot; and a large reed chest for the couple's wigs. There were also gold and lapis-lazuli necklaces, and leather and papyrus sandals showing signs of wear, as well as alabaster and pottery vessels, and food offerings. In addition, the splendid funerary equipment included the couple's beautiful deathmasks, amulets and scarabs, painted funerary papyri, canopic chests, and two enormous black-and-gold outer coffins containing gilded versions within. There were also *shabti* figures, each with its own shrine-shaped box; Yuya's was inscribed: "one in honor with Osiris, one favored by the good god [the king], Yuya, justified with the great god." The couple's mummies are extremely well preserved, indicating that the Egyptian embalmers had reached the very heights of their art.

This wooden goose-headed spoon with a lotus-flower bowl is inscribed for Mutemwia.

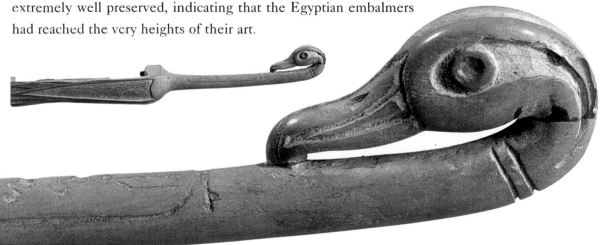

BEAUTY IN EXCHANGE FOR GOLD

YEAR 33 (ca. 1359BCE)

Amenhotep resolutely put aside his grief at the recent deaths in his family to concentrate on his duties as king, governing Egypt with a blend of hard politics and necessary ritual to maintain stability and peace. His astute dealings with fellow monarchs are brought into focus by a diplomatic archive of small clay tablets that was discovered inside a building at Amarna named the "office of the letters of Pharaoh." The tablets—inscribed in cuneiform script, the language of diplomacy—bring the players on the international stage vividly to life, revealing glimpses of their characters, from the opportunism of Kadashman-Enlil of Babylon to the warmth of Tushratta of Mitanni and the unexpected humor of Amenhotep himself.

Hathor, goddess of beauty and love, was often symbolized on objects belonging to women of the court. Among the animals that were sacred to Hathor was the ibex, which is used as a decorative element on this comb.

In their diplomatic correspondence with the Egyptian king, the great foreign potentates of Babylon, Mitanni, and Arzawa (southwestern Anatolia) had as their prime objective the acquisition of gold as Egypt had a reputation for great wealth. One letter states, "Gold is like the sand in Egypt, you simply gather it up." In exchange for this fabled Egyptian gold, foreign kings often gave their daughters and sisters, in what might almost seem like a straightforward business transaction. But the women were not necessarily sent against their will. One surviving letter from a princess, written in Babylonian, reads: "Say to my lord: so speaks the princess. For you, your chariots and your men, may all go well. May all the gods accompany you. In the presence of my lord I prostrate myself before you. My messenger brings you a gift of colored cloth. For your cities and your household may all go well. Do not worry, or you will have made me sad. I would give my life for you."

For Amenhotep, foreign marriages had a dual purpose. The king prized the beauty of his court women. Many of the daughters of his Egyptian officials and courtiers served as "royal ornaments": two stunning ladies appear in the tomb scenes of the royal scribe Menna. They wear fine linen robes adorned with jewelry of gold and precious stones, wide collars, large gold disk earrings, bracelets, and armlets, with copious hair spilling down over their kohl-rimmed eyes; appropriately they carry the sistrum, the sacred rattle of the goddess of love and beauty, Hathor. According to a contemporary love poem, the most beautiful woman of all "looks like the Morning Star, shining bright, fair of skin, lovely the look of her eyes and sweet the speech of her lips; upright neck, shining breast, hair of true lapis-lazuli ... with graceful steps she walks, and captures all hearts as she passes."

The arrival of foreign princesses at court had sound political benefits, too. Amenhotep was pursuing a well-established dynastic policy of securing international contacts by means of diplomatic marriage. His great-grandfather Tuthmosis III had taken three Syrian wives—Menhet, Menwi, and Merti—whom he honored with a sumptuous joint burial at Thebes. Amenhotep's father, Tuthmosis IV, had later sealed friendship with Mitanni through his marriage to a daughter of the Mitannian king Artatama I. In approximately 1382BCE Amenhotep III married Kiluhepa, daughter of Artatama's successor Shuttarna II. Twenty years later, when Tushratta was King of Mitanni, another diplomatic marriage was made between Amenhotep and Tushratta's daughter Taduhepa, Kiluhepa's niece.

Aside from his two Mitannian wives, Amenhotep made alliances with Arzawa and Babylon through marriage. By the later part of his reign he had three "great royal wives": Queen Tiy and their newly promoted daughters Sitamun and Isis. He also had five "minor" wives: Kiluhepa and Taduhepa of Mitanni; two unnamed Babylonian wives, daughters of Kurigalzu and his successor Kadashman-Enlil I; and the daughter of Tarkhundaradu, King of Arzawa.

Wedding negotiations could be protracted and involved the exchange of lavish "greeting gifts." When Kadashman-Enlil I of Babylon wrote asking for an

The household dwarf god Bes—who is depicted on this white faience cosmetic pot—was believed to bring good luck to couples and protect women during childbirth. He was also associated with the goddess Hathor and is often found on cosmetic items.

From the Theban tomb of Nebamun, a scribe and counter of grain, this detail of a wallpainting depicts members of the court of Amenhotep, who enjoyed the company of beautiful women. Amenhotep told one vassal in Asia Minor to "send very fair women—but none with shrill voices! Then the king your lord will say 'that is good!'"

Egyptian royal bride, he was refused and Amenhotep declared that, "From time immemorial, no daughter of the King of Egypt has ever been given to anyone." But the Babylonian pursued the issue, even suggesting an act of subterfuge: "Someone's grown-up daughters, beautiful women, must be available. So send me a beautiful woman as if she were your daughter and who will say, 'She is not the king's daughter?'" But Amenhotep simply repeated his refusal and there the matter ended.

Subsequently, when Amenhotep wrote asking to marry Kadashman-Enlil's daughter, the Babylonian was at first unforthcoming. But eventually he acceded to the request, writing, "My daughters being available, I will not refuse one to you," and adding in the very next sentence, "Now as to the gold I wrote to you about, send me whatever is on hand—as much as possible." Much of the lively correspondence between the two kings on this and other matters has survived (see opposite). Yet the flow of riches was not all in one direction: with his daughter Taduhepa, Tushratta King of Mitanni sent a necklace of gold and lapis-lazuli with the wish, "May it rest on the neck of my brother for one hundred thousand years," followed by a huge number of wedding gifts "of every sort."

In addition to the king's immediate female dependants and their children, who lived in quarters close to those of the king, there were at court more than 600 Mitannian women, as well as women from Syria, Asia Minor, and Palestine. They resided in their own part of the royal palace (the *ipet*), where they cared for their children, attended to their appearance, and produced textiles. They also played music, danced, and sang—not only for their own amusement and that of the king and the court, but as a vital part of ritual proceedings, for music and dance were integral to religious activity.

THE KING OF BABYLON TO AMENHOTEP III

"Say to Nimmuwareya [Nebmaatra], the king of Egypt, my brother: thus speaks Kadashman-Enlil, the king of Karaduniyash [Babylon]. For me and my country all goes very well. For you, your wives, your sons, your nobles, your horses, your chariots, and your entire country, may all go very well.

"You ask for my daughter in marriage, but my sister whom my father gave you was already there with you, and no one has seen her so as to know if she is alive or if she is dead. You addressed my messengers as your wives were standing gathered in your presence, saying, 'Here is your mistress who stands before you.' But my messengers did not know her, whether it was my sister who was at your side. My messengers did not know her. Who is to identify her? ... My daughters who are married to neighboring kings, if my messengers go there they speak with them, they send me a greeting gift. But the girl with you is poor."

AMENHOTEP III TO THE KING OF BABYLON

"Say to Kadashman-Enlil, the king of Karaduniyash, my brother: thus speaks Nebmaatra, the great king, the king of Egypt, your brother. For your household, your wives, your sons, your nobles, your horses, your chariots, your lands, may all go very well. For me all goes well. For my household, my wives, my sons, my nobles, my horses, my numerous troops, all goes well, and in my lands all goes very well ...

"Now, if your sister were dead, why would I conceal this fact and present someone else? As Amun is my witness, your sister is alive. I have made her a mistress of the household. You write: 'My daughters who are married to neighboring kings, if my messengers go there they speak with them, they send me a greeting gift. But the girl with you is poor.' These are your words ... Should your sister select some gift, I will send it to you! But it's a fine thing to give away your daughters just for the sake of acquiring a nugget of gold from your neighbors!"

THUS SPEAKS NIMMUWAREYA

Amenhotep III sent this "Amarna letter" —a small clay tablet inscribed in cuneiform script—to the Babylonian ruler Kadashman-Enlil. In the text the Egyptian king casts doubt on the credentials and honesty of the Babylonian envoys sent to his court.

In Amenhotep III's time, international diplomacy relied on messengers delivering communications from one monarch to another by hand across vast distances. Men such as the royal envoy Senu, May ("the king's messenger in every foreign land"), and envoys whose names were rendered Mane, Haaramashi, and Hane ("the interpreter") were sent through the empire to transmit the words of the Egyptian king to his fellow monarchs, his vassals, and his officials working abroad. Given the often sensitive nature of the political matters in question, those responsible for delivering the king's messages were chosen for their tact, honesty, and trustworthiness.

Ensuring safe passage was of the utmost importance. In the first letter that the Assyrian king Assuruballit despatched to Egypt, he declared: "I send my messenger to visit you and your country. Do not delay the messenger whom I send to you for a visit. He should visit and then return here. He should see what you are like and what your country is like and leave for here." When trying to justify his request for Egyptian gold, Assuruballit remarked: "We are countries far apart. Are our messengers to be always on the march with paltry results?" The men carried the precious clay tablets that bore their masters' communications around their necks; Amenhotep II referred to his interception of "a messenger from the king of Mitanni, with a clay letter at his neck" during his early military campaigns in Canaan. To ease their journeys these international postmen were provided with "passports"—messages guaranteeing their safe passage. The passport of a Mitannian messenger allowed him to go through Canaan into Egypt: "To the kings of Canaan, servants of my brother Nimmureya [Amenhotep III], thus speaks Tushratta. I herewith send Akiya, my messenger, to speed at once to the king

of Egypt my brother. No one is to delay him. Provide him safe passage into Egypt, and hand him over to the fortress commander on the Egyptian frontier. Let him go on, he is to owe nothing." Such international messages were written in Akkadian cuneiform, the diplomatic language of the era, in which the Egyptian king was referred to as "Nimmuwareya," "Nimmureya," "Nibmuareya," and other similar variants—the Akkadian versions of his throne name Nebmaatra. He was never known as Amenhotep in international correspondence. As a courtesy, and to emphasize their elevation above other men, the kings often addressed one another as "my brother."

Messengers often had to travel through inhospitable terrain and face great hazards. In his letter to Amenhotep, the Assyrian Assuruballit said: "As to your messengers having been delayed in reaching you, they had been pursued by Suteans and were in mortal danger. So I detained them until I could write to you, once I had ordered the Suteans be seized. So surely my messengers are not to be delayed in reaching me. Why should messengers be constantly made to stay out in the sun and so die in the sun? If staying in the sun means profit for the king, then let the messenger stay out and let him die right there in the sun, but for the king there must be a profit. Otherwise why should they die in the sun?" The Mitannian king Tushratta, impressed by the Egyptian messenger Mane and the interpreter Hane, treated them kindly. He wrote to Amenhotep: "I have exalted like gods my brother's messenger Mane, and Hane my brother's interpreter. I have given them many presents, and treated them very kindly, for their report was excellent … May my gods and the gods of my brother protect them."

It is clear that Amenhotep much preferred the Mitannian messengers— "chief minister" Keliya, Akiya, Tunip-ibri, and their interpreters—to those of the Babylonians, whom he regarded as untrustworthy and dishonest. He

In this detail of a restored painted scene from a Theban tomb, kneeling Nubian and Asiatic figures, visitors from the courts of foreign rulers, adorn the base of Amenhotep III's throne.

complained to Kadashman-Enlil I of Babylon: "Now we are brothers, you and I, but we have quarreled because of your messengers, since they report back to you saying, 'Nothing is given to us when we go to Egypt.' ... The first time the messengers went back to your father, their mouths told lies. The next time they went back to you, they told lies to you. So I said to myself, 'Whether I give them something or not they are going to carry on telling lies just the same.' So I made up my mind about them and I did not give them anything anymore ... Your messengers who have untruthful mouths and whom you sent here, I swear that they have not served you, and so they go on telling lies in order to escape your punishment." Amenhotep finished his letter with a further complaint: "As for your writing to me in order to benefit yourself ... you for your part sent me just one present. Are we to laugh?"

Given the strength of his feelings about the Babylonian messengers, it is unsurprising that Amenhotep had a tendency to keep them waiting—he allegedly did so for six years in one case. Kadashman-Enlil was driven to complain: "Previously my father would send a messenger to you, and you would not detain him for very long, quickly sending him off, and you would also send my father a beautiful greeting gift. But then when I sent that messenger to you, you detained him for six years, and sent me as a greeting gift—the only thing in six years—30 minas of gold that looked like silver!"

Kalbaya, messenger of Tarkhundaradu of Arzawa, was not always trusted, even by his own king, who wrote to Amenhotep: "My messenger Kalbaya has spoken these words to me, 'Let us establish a blood-relationship.' In this matter I do not trust Kalbaya. He has indeed spoken it as a word, but it was not confirmed on the tablet. If you really desire my daughter, why should I not give her to you? I give her to you! See to it now that Kalbaya returns quickly, and write back to me on a tablet concerning this matter."

The sending of the daughters of foreign kings to the Egyptian court was strictly one-way traffic. In the single instance when a monarch—Kadashman-Enlil I—had the temerity to ask for an Egyptian bride, he was absolutely refused (see pages 147–148).

Many children from foreign vassal states were sent to Egypt to be raised and educated with the pharaoh's offspring, but also, no doubt, to act as bargaining counters in the diplomatic game. A stela that once stood in Amenhotep's funerary temple reported that the temple buildings "are filled with children of the princes of every foreign land that his majesty has seized."

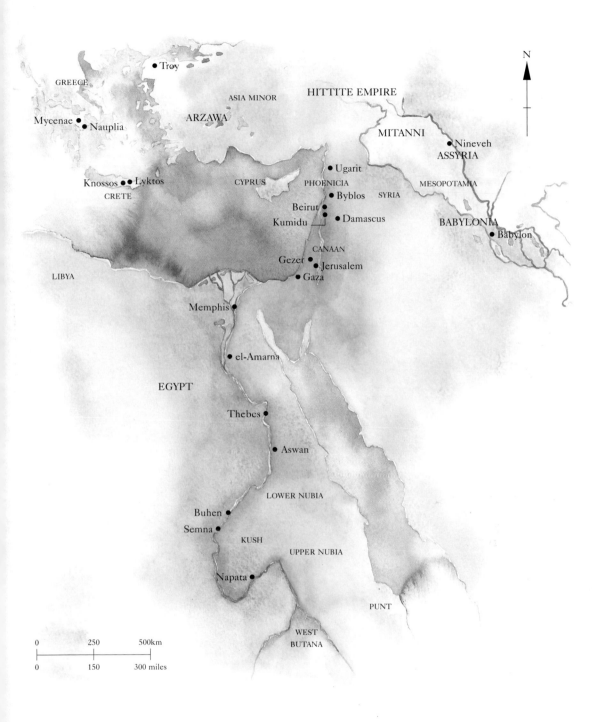

This map of the Eastern Mediterranean and Near East during
the reign of Amenhotep III shows the extent of the Egyptian
empire and the other kingdoms with which Amenhotep was
in contact. The distances their messengers had to cover were
often vast: envoys had to travel for many weeks through terrain
that was frequently hostile and hazardous.

THE LIVING SUN

YEARS 34–35 (ca. 1358–1357BCE)

In ca. 1358BCE Amenhotep celebrated his second *sed* or jubilee festival, splendidly attired and wearing the dual red-and-white crown that symbolized dominion over a united Egypt. After his first *sed*, held in ca. 1362BCE to mark thirty years of rule, Amenhotep wore increasing amounts of gold jewelry, whose glittering in the Egyptian sunlight must have given him the qualities of the sun itself—a golden ruler emanating golden rays. As part of this second *sed*, the king made his second daughter, Isis, a "great royal wife," replacing the late Mutemwia. This brought the number of great royal wives back up to three.

This solid-gold figurine of a king holding the royal crook and flail was discovered in Tutankhamun's tomb inside a miniature coffin, which also contained a lock of Queen Tiy's hair. Some experts believe the figurine may represent Amenhotep III.

The stage-managed *sed* festival presented the king, dressed in magnificent clothes and jewelry, as an impressive figure. As his reign progressed, Amenhotep experimented with his ceremonial robes, moving on from a close-fitting jubilee cloak with fringed borders to an elaborately pleated garment. It was part of a more general trend in which the king's costume became increasingly ornate. He had almost always worn a necklace of some sort, but the wide floral *wah* collars and beaded *weskhet* collars of his early years extended over the entire shoulder in these latter stages of his reign. The king also began to wear heavier pectoral pendants—the same type of grandiose jewelry that was found in the tomb of his grandson Tutankhamun, some of which had been reworked, which implies it had previously belonged to another royal figure. Amenhotep sometimes wore three of his thick gold *shebyu* necklaces at a time, together with gold armlets and bracelets.

Laden with such heavy regalia during the *sed*'s lengthy ritual proceedings, the king would have been thankful for the services of men such as Maiherpri and Amenmosi, both "fan-bearers on the king's right hand." Many finely crafted, feathered fans have survived—both long-handled ceremonial ones known as *shuwt* and short-handled personal ones called *khuw*. Tutankhamun was buried with eight fans, the smallest of which still retains its soft feathers.

In ca. 1357BCE the great granary at Karnak was completed. It housed the god Amun-Ra's share of the abundant grain that was produced by a succession of good harvests—a direct reflection of Amenhotep's divine powers. The painted sandstone reliefs set into the mudbrick walls of the granary show the king finely dressed in a kilt with an elaborate apron. He is adorned with a golden collar, a double *shebyu* necklace, and six golden armlets, as well as a great solar crown of pendant uraei snakes and sun disks on his head. He also wears an innovative style of wig: it is the standard rounded shape, but its fringed layers frame the face and draw attention to royal features that are now depicted as youthful in their beauty and roundness.

At the Soleb temple in Upper Nubia, Amenhotep III was worshiped alongside Amun-Ra as "Nebmaatra, lord of Nubia" with the powers of the moon god. The temple's sandstone relief portrays the *sed*-festival rites during which Amenhotep was deified as the sun god, wearing the horns of Amun-Ra and a crown of combined solar and lunar disks.

THE SCRIBE WHO BECAME A GOD

In ca. 1358BCE the king lost his trusted official Amenhotep son of Hapu, who had risen from a temple scribe to become Egypt's pre-eminent official (see pages 98–99). After his death the scribe was eventually revered as a god.

We know from a statue of the scribe from Karnak temple that he had attained an astonishing age (for antiquity) and had ambitions for a longer life still: "I have reached the age of 80 years, I am greatly praised by the king, and I will complete 110 years." The inscription goes on to describe the official's desire to "go out into the sky and be united with the stars, acclaimed in the boat of the sun god." Amenhotep son of Hapu was buried with great reverence in a rock-cut tomb near Qurnet Murai in the Theban hills. The king also provided the scribe with his own funerary temple close to the royal one, an honor usually reserved for monarchs.

The cult of Amenhotep son of Hapu was endowed and protected by royal decree, a declaration that was witnessed by vizier Amenhotep and "overseer of the gold house" Meriptah. The decree proved effective indeed. The cult of Hapu's son was still functioning centuries after his death, when that of the king he had served so devotedly was a mere memory.

A black-granite statue from Karnak temple shows the aged scribe Amenhotep son of Hapu wearing a long, high-waisted kilt.

A GODDESS COMES
TO THEBES

YEAR 36 (ca. 1356BCE)

In ca. 1356BCE King Tushratta of Mitanni despatched to Egypt a statue of Ishtar, the Babylonian goddess of love and fertility, to mark the marriage of his daughter Taduhepa to Amenhotep. Tushratta wrote: "I have given my daughter to be the wife of my brother whom I love. May the gods make her the image of my brother's desire. May my brother rejoice on that day. May Ishtar grant my brother great blessings and exquisite joy. May the gods bless him and may you, my brother, live for ever."

It has generally been assumed that Tushratta sent the statue of the goddess to cure Amenhotep of an ailment from which he must have been suffering, but there is no evidence for this. It seems most likely that Ishtar—"Sausga" to the Mitannians—was sent to bless the union of Egypt and Mitanni. More than 20 years earlier, Tushratta's father Shuttarna II had sent a statue of Ishtar to Egypt with his daughter Kiluhepa and her 317 waiting-women (see page 62). Now Tushratta wrote: "Thus says Ishtar of Nineveh, lady of every land, 'I wish to go to Egypt, a country I love, then return.' So now I send her, and she is on her way. In the time of my father, Ishtar went to your country, and just as earlier she lived there and they honored her, so now may my brother honor her ten times more than before. May my brother honor her, then at his pleasure let her go so that she may come back to us. May Ishtar, mistress of heaven, protect us, my brother and me, for one hundred thousand years, and may our mistress give both of us great joy. And let us remain friends."

Ishtar's statue would have traveled south to Egypt in her golden shrine, accompanied, no doubt, by Tushratta's most trusted messenger, chief minister Keliya, and a great entourage. When she arrived in Thebes, to the acclaim of the crowds, the atmosphere must have been similar to that of the Egyptian Hathor festival, when the goddess's statue was taken out of her temple into the daylight and presented to the people to celebrate another successful harvest. Similar proceedings also marked the wedding-like atmosphere each year when Hathor's statue was removed from its temple at Dendera to spend two weeks in the sacred company of her husband Horus in his temple at Edfu.

Attended by a great retinue of priests and priestesses, musicians and dancers, Ishtar's statue would have joined with that of Amun-Ra in order to bless the royal union. It was hoped that Ishtar's powers as a goddess of sexuality and fertility—celebrated for her sweet lips and beautiful figure—would be transferred to Taduhepa, giving her the capacity to satisfy her new husband's desire and bring divine blessings on Amenhotep's palace, his people, and his realm.

This 8th-century BCE Babylonian relief shows the goddess Ishtar riding on the back of a lion.

As well as being a love goddess, Ishtar also had a violent aspect: known as "the lady of battles," she possessed considerable aggressive powers, and rode with kings fully armed into battle to destroy their enemies' weapons. In this aspect Ishtar was represented by the lioness, and her image was strikingly similar to that of Hathor, whose benign beauty could at any time be transformed into the vengeful force of the lioness Sekhmet.

Ishtar was the counterpart of the Syrian goddess Astarte, who, by the era of the New Kingdom, had been absorbed into the cosmopolitan Egyptian pantheon. As a combative daughter of the sun god Ra, Astarte was closely associated with the skills of chariotry. The inscription on Amenhotep II's Sphinx stela declares that she was particularly impressed by the young prince's prowess in this pursuit: "Astarte rejoiced over him." Astarte's sexual powers were embodied by the Syrian goddess Qadesh, who was believed to ride naked on the back of a lion. Qadesh's cult involved her devotees enthusiastically simulating the sacred marriage between the goddess and her male equivalent (the god Reshep).

AMENHOTEP THE MAGNIFICENT

YEAR 37 (ca. 1355BCE)

A s Amenhotep enjoyed newly married bliss with his young Mitannian wife Taduhepa, Egypt basked in the golden glow of its pharaoh and an era of peace and prosperity that it seemed would last for ever. Building work was well under way to extend the already sprawling royal palace at Malkata, no doubt to accommodate Taduhepa's recently arrived entourage of 270 women and 30 men and the king's ever-increasing household of women and children. The god-king chose the thirty-seventh year of his reign to reaffirm his regal powers with a third *sed* festival, just three years after the previous one.

Found at Karnak, this small stucco head shows Amenhotep III wearing the blue war crown. He is portrayed with the rejuvenated, childlike features associated with the three *sed* festivals held during the last decade of his reign.

Scenes in the Theban tomb of Kheruef commemorate the events of the third *sed*. Bedecked in golden necklaces, collars, armlets, and bracelets, the king celebrates the festival in a blue war crown, kilt, and sandals, with the traditional bull's tail attached to the back of his kilt to symbolize power and strength. Amenhotep is depicted hauling on ropes in order to raise a great *djed* pillar, representing stability as the backbone of Osiris. The great royal wife Tiy looks on, holding her scepters, while the king's other wives and daughters shake their sistra in encouragement; they are identified in the inscription as "the king's children who propitiate the august *djed* pillar."

By the time of the third *sed*, Sobekmose had been succeeded by his son Sobekhotep "Panehesy" ("the Nubian") as overseer of the treasury. The new appointee's first task was to make an expedition into Sinai to the mines at Serabit el-Khadim "to fetch turquoise while his majesty was preparing to celebrate the *sed* festival for the third time." Sobekhotep commemorated his achievements at Serabit el-Khadim by setting up two large stelae inside the temple of Hathor, "Lady of the Turquoise."

Another Sinai inscription refers to the important trade in gum resin, describing how an official delegation was sent "to the sea coast to announce the marvels of Punt (Somalia), to receive the aromatic gum brought by the chiefs as tribute from the lands one did not know." The aromatic gum resins frankincense, myrrh, and pistacia were imported from the earliest times, mainly from the territory to the south of Egypt around modern Somalia. The Egyptians used large quantities of the resins as incense for ritual purposes in both temples and tombs; frankincense found in the tomb of Tutankhamun was used during his funeral ceremonies as incense and during his mummification.

Resins were also used in perfume production, together with moringa oil, used as a sweet-smelling hair preparation by male city-dwellers of the New Kingdom. Three wooden labels from Amenhotep III's tomb bear hieratic inscriptions referring to moringa oil that had been produced specifically for the third *sed* festival. Another docket dated Year 37, found in the royal tomb's nearby storeroom, indicates that at this time funerary goods were being collected in preparation for Amenhotep III's eventual burial.

The scarab pectoral of Amenhotep's grandson Tutankhamun is made of gold inlaid with lapis-lazuli, cornelian, green feldspar, and turquoise from the Sinai mines. This piece was found in the treasury of Tutankhamun's lavish tomb in the Valley of the Kings.

THE ATEN IS DEAD, LONG LIVE THE ATEN

YEAR 38 (ca. 1354BCE)

Seven months into his thirty-eighth year as king, probably in January 1354BCE, Amenhotep III died. The most likely cause of death was old age—he had lived to almost 50 at a time when average life expectancy in Egypt was around 35. As his grief-stricken subjects began the traditional 70-day period of mourning, Amenhotep's body would have been taken in state from Malkata along the causeway, north to his massive funerary temple at Kom el-Hetan (see pages 142–143).

The mummy of Amenhotep III was damaged by tomb-robbers, but was rewrapped during the 21st Dynasty before its reburial in the tomb of his grandfather Amenhotep II.

At the temple the king's body was washed and purified before being taken to the myrrh-scented "house of beauty," in which embalmers such as Tuthmosis ("Paroy"), "head of the secrets in the chest of Anubis," as he is called in inscriptions in his Theban tomb, undertook the elaborate rituals of mummification. Once eviscerated, the royal body was desiccated beneath piles of dry natron, then washed, anointed with lavish quantities of perfumed oils, and adorned with jewelry of gold and precious stones, his fingers and toes covered with thimble-like gold covers to keep his nails in place. To the intoning of funerary texts, the body was wrapped in great quantities of fine linen, each layer interspersed with protective amulets. The head was covered by a gold deathmask and, after further anointing, covered in flowers, including floral *wah* collars. Thus prepared, Amenhotep's mummy was placed within its nest of golden coffins and laid in its golden shrine to await the funeral.

One morning sometime in March, the viziers and highest officials, dressed in plain white robes and headbands, assembled to take the king to

his final resting place. Accompanied by the eldest son and heir, Prince Amenhotep, with the great royal wives Tiy, Sitamun, and Isis acting as chief mourners, and all the king's officials and attendants carrying funerary goods, the cortege left the temple. Passing the smaller temples of Amenhotep's predecessors, it turned into the silence of the Western Valley. Here the king's great tomb awaited him, its chambers filled with the contents of its nearby storeroom, including chariots, archery equipment, wooden shrines, statues of the gods, food and wine, cosmetics and perfumes, model boats, sandals, and fans.

The head of one of the alabaster (calcite) *shabti* figures of Amenhotep III, found in his West Valley tomb, shows the king wearing the royal *nemes* headcloth and uraeus.

At the tomb the funerary rituals were performed amid clouds of purifying incense. The dead king's mouth, eyes, ears, and nose were symbolically reopened with ritual implements in a ceremony designed to reawaken all his senses, and he was sated with offerings as the standard formula was recited for "a thousand jars of perfume, incense, unguent, and all kinds of herbs, all kinds of offerings on which the gods live." Amenhotep was then exhorted to "Live again! You have become young again! You are young again, for ever!" Once the king's soul had been reawoken, his mummy was taken into the burial chamber deep within his tomb, where it was placed in a massive red-granite sarcophagus, covered in gold and decorated with *wedjat* eyes, the sky goddess Nut, and the words of Osiris, lord of the afterlife: "My son, Nebmaatra, my beloved heir, Amenhotep, ruler of Thebes, you have come together with the gods, and I have given to you the necropolis of the West."

When the funerary rituals had been completed, the pharaoh's eldest surviving son became his successor. Named after his father, Amenhotep IV—who later took the name Akhenaten, "one beneficial to the Aten"—ascended the throne of Upper and Lower Egypt. All hoped the golden era of his father would continue; foreign powers held their breath as the world's greatest nation passed through its period of transition. Tushratta of Mitanni had been grief-stricken on being told of Amenhotep's death: "When I heard that my brother Nimmuwareya had gone to his fate, on that day I sat down and wept. On that day I took no food, I took no water." Now he could only hope that his special relationship with Egypt would continue. "When they told me that Naphureya, eldest son of Nimmuwareya and Teye [Tiy] his principal wife, is king in his place, I said, 'Nimmuwareya my brother is not dead! Naphureya his eldest son is in his place, and nothing whatsoever will ever be changed from the way it was before.'"

But Tushratta's hopes were unfounded, for Amenhotep IV was but a pale imitation of the dazzling father he tried to emulate. He began by taking over his father's household, including the most recent royal wife, his step-mother Taduhepa. Queen Tiy, who lived on for at least another eight years, acted as effective regent for a son who never seemed to have much of a grasp of political reality. In her attempts to guide the young king, she took over diplomatic correspondence, asking the king of Mitanni to remember the love he had borne her husband and increase it now for her son. Tushratta for his part

CULT OF THE SUN KING

Amenhotep III's reign saw great emphasis on the sun in all its aspects. The supreme ancient solar deity Ra had been combined with Amun to create Amun-Ra, and worshiped together with the solar creator god Atum, Khepri, and Horus as gods of the rising sun and the Aten sun disk. For the first time, the Aten was provided with its own priesthood and its own temple built in the traditional solar capital of Heliopolis, and throughout the reign there were countless references to this "new" god. The king's own favorite epithet was *Aten-tjehen*, "dazzling Aten."

Amenhotep II and his son Tuthmosis IV had begun the process of regenerating the ancient solar cult that had existed 1,000 years before under the pyramid-building monarchy of the Old Kingdom. The steps Tuthmosis had taken to distance the throne from the Karnak

clergy of Amun and so curtail its growing powers were taken much further by Amenhotep III, who skillfully manipulated the Amun cult for his own ends while promoting the sun god Ra in the form of the Aten (see pages 60–61).

In contemporary Egyptian belief the pharaoh rose up at death and merged with the Aten. However, in the case of Amenhotep III, it seems that the king actually became the Aten, rather than simply being absorbed by it.

This painted limestone stela features relief figures of Amenhotep III and Tiy seated before plentiful offerings. Carved in typical "Amarna style," it was originally in the domestic shrine in the house of Akhenaten's official Panehesy.

wrote to the new king urging him to consult Tiy on matters of state, since she was the only one who knew Amenhotep III's policies in detail.

But Amenhotep IV seems not to have heeded this advice; in his attempts to reduce expenditure he offended the Mitannians by substituting gold-plated statues for the solid-gold ones promised by Amenhotep III to Tushratta just before he died. The new king also relocated the Egyptian capital far to the north in the backwaters of Middle Egypt, where he built the completely new but relatively short-lived Akhetaten, "Horizon of the Aten" (Tell el-Amarna).

The reign of Amenhotep III had been momentous. The king became the standard against whom all subsequent pharaohs measured themselves. His name featured prominently in later king lists and he appeared as a figure of veneration in later Ramesside tomb scenes. This reputation continued into the classical period, when the greatest attraction for visiting tourists, including the Roman emperors Hadrian and Septimius Severus, were the two colossal "Memnon" figures of the king (see page 142). The admiration of early European scholars was based on the great quality and quantity of items bearing Amenhotep III's name: his monuments were the focus of the great French scholarly expedition of 1799.

Amenhotep III's glowing reputation suffered at the hands of Victorian and early 20th-century scholars, however. After the discovery of objects at Amarna that portray Amenhotep and the rest of the royal family in the highly exaggerated Amarna style of art, he was dismissed out of hand as a languid monarch whose life was given over to pleasure and self-glorification. He was even blamed for the later failings of his son. Volumes written about Akhenaten credited him with being a revolutionary in religion and art when in fact his father had led the way years before. But antiquated scholarly notions are now being reassessed in the light of a vast amount of recent research that looks set to reinstate Amenhotep III in his rightful place as probably the most significant ruler of the entire pharaonic period. In modern Egypt, Amenhotep III is still celebrated in folk memory; his name is heard in songs of modern Egyptian schoolchildren and particularly among the people of Qurna, who live amid the beautiful tombs of Amenhotep's courtiers. Gathering at the feet of the Colossi of Memnon to have their wedding photographs taken, perhaps only a few visitors realize that they stand on the threshold of what was once the greatest temple in Egypt, its builder the greatest pharaoh of them all, Amenhotep, ruler of Thebes.

OVERLEAF A detail from the funerary papyrus of the 18th-Dynasty scribe
Nebked, showing him making offerings to Osiris, lord of the afterlife.

PHARAOH'S PEOPLE

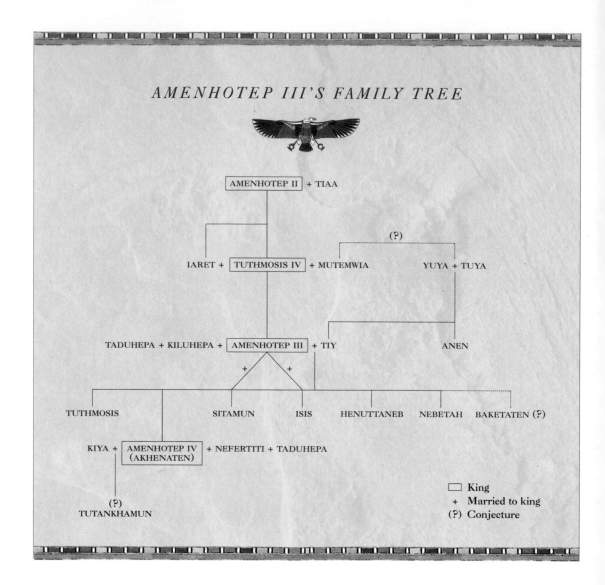

AMENHOTEP III'S FAMILY TREE

AMENHOTEP II + TIAA

IARET + TUTHMOSIS IV + MUTEMWIA   (?)   YUYA + TUYA

TADUHEPA + KILUHEPA + AMENHOTEP III + TIY   ANEN

+   +

TUTHMOSIS   SITAMUN   ISIS   HENUTTANEB   NEBETAH   BAKETATEN (?)

KIYA + AMENHOTEP IV + NEFERTITI + TADUHEPA
        (AKHENATEN)

☐ King
+ Married to king
(?) Conjecture

(?)
TUTANKHAMUN

KING AMENHOTEP III
Amenhotep III's royal names:
Birth name ("son of Ra" name): Amen-hotep heka-Waset ("Amenhotep, ruler of Thebes")
Throne name ("king of Upper and Lower Egypt" name): Neb-maat-ra ("Ra, lord of truth")
Horus name: Ka-nakht kha-em -ma'at ("strong bull, appearing in truth")
Two Ladies name: Semen-hepu segereh-tawy ("he who establishes laws and pacifies the Two Lands")
Golden Horus name: Aa-khepesh hu-Setiu ("great of strength, smiter of the Asiatics")

Aakheperure, possible brother of Amenhotep III
Amenemhat, brother of Amenhotep III
Amenemipet, sister of Amenhotep III
Amenhotep II, grandfather of Amenhotep III, father of Tuthmosis IV

Amenhotep IV (Akhenaten), second son of Amenhotep III and Tiy

Amenhotep son of Hapu, royal scribe; scribe of recruits; overseer of all works; overseer of priests of Horus Khenty-khety of Athribis

Amenhotep Huy, southern vizier; overseer of all works of the king

Amenhotep Huy, chief steward in Memphis; overseer of the treasury; controller of works in Ptah temple; scribe of recruits; overseer of priests; military officer

Anen, Queen Tiy's brother, second prophet of Amun; lector priest; *sem* priest; seal-bearer of the king

Baketaten, daughter of Amenhotep III and Tiy

Hatiay, granary overseer of the mansion of the Aten

Heby, mayor of Memphis; overseer of the cattle of Amun; overseer of granaries of Amun; father of Vizier Ramose

Henuttaneb, daughter of Amenhotep III and Tiy

Hor, twin brother of Suti; overseer of works of Amun in Southern Ipet

Iaret, sister and great royal wife of Tuthmosis IV

Iny, daughter of Amenhotep III

Isis, daughter of Amenhotep III and Tiy; great royal wife of Amenhotep III

Kadashman-Enlil I, King of Babylon; father of an unnamed wife of Amenhotep III

Khaemhat (nicknamed "Mahu"), overseer of the two granaries of Upper and Lower Egypt

Khaemwaset, overseer of northern countries

Kheruef (nicknamed "Senaa"), Queen Tiy's steward; royal scribe

Kiluhepa, daughter of Shuttarna II of Mitanni; minor wife of Amenhotep III

Kiya, minor wife of Amenhotep IV

Merymose, viceroy of Kush; overseer of the gold lands of Amun

Meryptah, high priest of Amun; overseer of priests of all gods

Meryra, chancellor; chief steward of the king when a child; overseer of king's nurses

Mutemwia, minor wife of Tuthmosis IV, mother of Amenhotep III (who gave her the title of king's mother, great royal wife and god's mother)

Nebetah, daughter of Amenhotep III and Tiy

Nefertiry, great royal wife of Tuthmosis IV

Nefertiti, great royal wife of Amenhotep IV (Akhenaten) and his possible successor

Petepihu, sister of Amenhotep III

Ptahmose, chancellor; high priest of Ptah in Memphis

Ptahmose, southern vizier; high priest of Amun; overseer of all works; mayor of Thebes; overseer of priests of Upper and Lower Egypt; fan-bearer on the king's right hand; steward of Amun

Ramose, northern vizier; overseer of priests of Upper and Lower Egypt

Shuttarna II, king of Mitanni and father of Kiluhepa

Siatum, royal prince, possible brother of Amenhotep III

Sitamun, eldest daughter of Amenhotep III and Tiy; great royal wife of Amenhotep III

Sobekhotep, chief treasurer of Tuthmosis IV; mayor of Fayuum; guardian of Amenhotep III when a child

Suti, twin brother of Hor; overseer of works of the king in Thebes

Taduhepa, daughter of Tushratta of Mitanni; minor wife of Amenhotep III; minor wife of Amenhotep IV (Akhenaten)

Tiaa, great royal wife of Amenhotep II; mother of Tuthmosis IV

Tiaa, sister of Amenhotep III

Tinetamun, sister of Amenhotep III

Tiy, great royal wife of Amenhotep III

Tushratta, King of Mitanni; father of Taduhepa

Tutankhamun, possible grandson of Amenhotep III

Tuthmosis IV, father of Amenhotep III

Tuthmosis, Crown Prince, eldest son of Amenhotep III and Tiy; high priest of Ptah; overseer of priests of Upper and Lower Egypt; *sem* priest

Tuthmosis (nicknamed "Paroy"), *sem* priest in the good house; embalmer

Tuya, Queen Tiy's mother; chief of entertainers of Amun and Min; singer of Amun and Hathor

Yuya, Queen Tiy's father; priest of Min; overseer of the cattle of Min; master of the horse; royal commander of chariotry

FURTHER READING

Aldred, C. *Akhenaten, King of Egypt*. Thames & Hudson: London, 1988.

Arnold, D., Green, L., and Allen, J. *The Royal Women of Amarna: Images of Beauty from Ancient Egypt*. Metropolitan Museum of Art: New York, 1996.

Baines, J. and Malék, J. *Atlas of Ancient Egypt*. Phaidon: Oxford, 1980.

Berman, L. M., ed. *The Art of Amenhotep III: Art Historical Analysis*. Cleveland Museum of Art: Cleveland, 1990.

Brovarski, E., et al. *Egypt's Golden Age: The Art of Living in the New Kingdom, 1558–1085BC*. Museum of Fine Arts, Boston: Boston, 1982.

Bryan, B. M. *The Reign of Thutmose IV*. John Hopkins University Press: Baltimore, 1991.

Fletcher, J. *Ancient Egypt: Life, Myth, and Art*. Duncan Baird Publishers: London, 1999; Stewart, Tabori & Chang: New York, 1999.

Forbes, C. and Garner, G. *Documents of the Egyptian Empire*. Australian Institute of Archaeology: Melbourne, 1982.

Gardiner, A. *Egypt of the Pharaohs*. Oxford University Press: Oxford, 1961.

Goedicke, H. *Problems concerning Amenophis III*. Halgo: Baltimore, 1992.

Goring, E., et al., eds. *Chief of Seers: Egyptian studies in memory of Cyril Aldred*. Kegan Paul International: London, 1997.

Harris, J. and Wente, E. *An X-Ray Atlas of the Royal Mummies*. University of Chicago Press: Chicago, 1980.

Hart, G. *A Dictionary of Egyptian Gods & Goddesses*. Routledge & Kegan Paul: London, 1986.

Hayes, W. *The Scepter of Egypt II*. Abrams: New York, 1959.

James, T. G. H. and Davies, W. V. *Egyptian Sculpture*. British Museum Press: London, 1983.

Kemp, B. J. *Ancient Egypt: Anatomy of a Civilization*. Routledge: London, 1989.

Kozloff, A. and Bryan, B. *Egypt's Dazzling Sun: Amenhotep III and his World*. Cleveland Museum of Art: Cleveland, 1992.

Lacovara, P. *The New Kingdom Royal City*. Kegan Paul International: London, 1997.

Lesko, L. *King Tut's Wine Cellar*. B.C. Scribe Publications: Albany, 1977.

Lichtheim, M. *Ancient Egyptian Literature* (3 volumes). University of California Press: Berkeley, 1980.

Moran, W. L. *The Amarna Letters*. John Hopkins University Press: Baltimore, 1992.

O'Connor, D. and Cline, E. H., eds. *Amenhotep III: Perspectives on his Reign*. University of Michigan Press: Michigan, 1998.

Pendlebury, J. D. S., et al. *The City of Akhenaten III*, (2 volumes). Egypt Exploration Society: London, 1951.

Reeves, N. and Wilkinson, R. H. *The Complete Valley of the Kings*. Thames & Hudson: London, 1996.

Riefstahl, E. *Thebes in the Time of Amenhotep III*. University of Oklahoma Press: Oklahoma, 1964.

Roberts, A. *Hathor Rising: the Serpent Power of Ancient Egypt*. Northgate: Devon, 1995.

Romer, J. *Valley of the Kings*. Michael O'Mara: London, 1981.

Shafer, B. E., ed. *Temples of Ancient Egypt*. I. B. Tauris: London, 1998.

Silverman, David P., ed. *Ancient Egypt*. Duncan Baird Publishers: London, 1997; Oxford University Press: New York, 1997.

Smith, W. Stevenson. *The Art & Architecture of Ancient Egypt*. Pelican: Harmondsworth, England, 1981.

Trigger, B. G., Kemp, B. J., O'Connor, D. B., and Lloyd, A. B. *Ancient Egypt: A Social History*. Cambridge University Press: Cambridge, 1983.

Vogelsang-Eastwood, G. *Tutankhamun's Wardrobe*. Barjesteh van Waalwijk van Doorn & Co, Rotterdam, 1999.

Wildung, D. *Egyptian Saints: Deification in Pharaonic Egypt*. New York University Press: New York, 1977.

GLOSSARY

Amarna period Traditional term for the reign of Amenhotep III's son, Akhenaten, who moved the court to el-Amarna.

amulet A protective charm.

ankh The symbol for "life."

atef **crown** A plumed crown worn by the pharaoh on certain ritual occasions.

Aten, the The disk or orb of the sun, which came to be worshiped as a god.

barque shrine Shrine in the shape of a boat dedicated to a particular deity.

Book of the Dead, the Funerary texts comprising spells for ensuring safe passage to the afterlife.

canopic jars Four stone or ceramic vessels in which the entrails of a mummified corpse were stored.

cartouche A protective oval-shaped outline, which, from the Fourth Dynasty onward, was drawn around the king's birth name and throne name.

cataracts Rocky areas of rapids in the mid Nile valley.

cubit An ancient unit of measurement based on the length of a forearm.

djed **pillar** A symbol of stability representing the backbone of Osiris.

faience Glazed ceramic, usually bright blue in color.

harem Literally "private quarters," the living area of women and children.

ka An individual's soul or life-force.

Middle Kingdom The second great era of Egyptian civilization (ca. 2040–1640BCE), covering the Eleventh to Thirteenth dynasties of pharaohs.

natron A naturally occurring salt compound used in purification and in the drying of the body during mummification.

nemes **headcloth** The striped headcloth worn by pharaohs.

New Kingdom The third and greatest era of Egyptian civilization (ca.1539–1075BCE), covering the Eighteenth to Twentieth dynasties of pharaohs.

nomes The administrative districts into which Upper and Lower Egypt were divided.

Old Kingdom The first great era of Egyptian civilization (ca. 2625–2130BCE), covering the Third to Sixth dynasties of pharaohs.

Pharaoh The king of Egypt, a Greek term derived from the Egyptian *per-aa* ("Great House"), which originally referred to the royal palace but from the New Kingdom onward (see above) was also used to mean the ruler.

pylon The monumental gateway of an Egyptian temple.

sed **festival (or *heb-sed*)** The royal jubilee festival and ritual of renewal and regeneration, traditionally celebrated by a pharaoh after 30 years of rule. Amenhotep held three during the last decade of his reign.

sem **priest** A priest who performed the "opening of the mouth" ceremony during funeral rites.

shabti Small funerary figures whose purpose was to serve the deceased in the afterlife.

shebyu **collar** A gold collar of honor awarded by the king to officials in recognition of service.

stela A flat piece of stone or wood bearing inscriptions or reliefs.

tyet The symbol of the sacred knot of Isis.

uraeus The image of the sacred serpent, or cobra, usually placed over the royal brow so that it could spit into the eyes of the king's enemies.

Valley of the Kings A royal burial ground on the West Bank of the Nile, containing the tombs of pharaohs.

Valley of the Queens A cemetery of royal wives and sons of some New Kingdom pharaohs, located south of the Valley of the Kings.

waab **priest** A priest who was ritually purified.

wah **collar** A wide floral collar.

wedjat **eye** Protective eye of Horus used as an amulet.

West Valley A separate part of the New Kingdom royal necropolis known as the Valley of the Kings (see above) at Thebes. The tomb of King Amenhotep III is located in the West Valley.

INDEX

PICTURE CREDITS

The publishers would like to thank the photographers and organizations for their kind permission to reproduce the following photographs in this book:

KEY

t top; **b** bottom; **c** center; l left; **r** right

AKG	AKG London
ÄM	Ägyptisches Museum, Staatliche Museen Preussischer Kulturbesitz, Berlin
BAL	Bridgeman Art Library, London
BM	British Museum, London
EM	Egyptian Museum, Cairo
ET	e.t. archive, London
JL	Jürgen Liepe Photo Archive, Berlin
ML	Musée du Louvre, Paris
RHPL	Robert Harding Picture Library, London
RMN	Réunion des Musées Nationaux, Paris
WFA	Werner Forman Archive, London

Front cover: WFA/ÄM; **2** Tony Stone Images, London/John Lawrence; **3** BM; **6** WFA/Luxor Museum of Ancient Egyptian Art; **8–9** BAL/ Giraudon/ML; **10** Victoria & Albert Museum, London; **11** RHPL/Walter Rawlings/EM; **12** Peter Clayton, Hertfordshire; **14** Kunsthistorisches Museum, Vienna; **16** Joann Fletcher; **17** Scala, Florence/EM; **19** RHPL/Simon Harris; **21** ÄM/ Margarete Büsing; **23** Axiom, London/

James Morris; **24** Joann Fletcher; **25** ET/BM; **26** BM; **27** Joann Fletcher/ BM; **28** BAL/BM; **29** JL/EM; **30–31** BM; **32** Peter Clayton; **33** Scala, Florence; **34** Kestner Museum, Hanover/Olaf M Tessmer; **37** RHPL/FL Kenett; **38** Earl of Carnarvon, Highclere Castle, Berkshire; **39** AKG/BM; **43** BAL/ML; **45** Joachim Willeitner, Munich; **46** ET/EM; **47** Scala, Florence/ Museo Civico, Bologna; **48–9** Joachim Willeitner, Munich; **50** Museo Egizio, Turin; **51** Joachim Willeitner, Munich; **52** JL/EM; **53** BAL/ML; **54** George B Johnson, Ohio; **55** WFA/ÄM; **56** RMN/ML/Hervé Lewandowski; **57** Graham Harrison/Luxor Museum of Ancient Egyptian Art; **58** BM; **59** BM; **60** EM; **62tl** BM; **62tr** BM; **63t** BM; **63b** ET/EM; **66–7** WFA/Dr E Strouhal; **68** JL/EM; **69** Musées Royaux d'Art et d'Histoire, Brussels; **71** ET/EM; **72** RMN/ML/Hervé Lewandowski; **73** WFA/ÄM; **75** BM; **77** JL/EM; **78** BM; **80** BAL/Brooklyn Museum of Art, New York; **81b** RMN/ML/Lebée; **83** Graham Harrison, Oxfordshire; **84** BM; **86–7c** AKG/Erich Lessing; **89** AKG/ Erich Lessing; **90** Earl of Carnarvon, Highclere Castle, Berkshire; **91** AKG/Museo Egizio, Turin/Erich Lessing; **93** AKG/Erich Lessing; **94** ÄM/ Margarete Büsing; **95** WFA; **96–7** BAL/BM; **99** JL/EM; **100** JL/EM; **103** Scala, Florence; **104–5** WFA/Luxor Museum of Ancient Egyptian Art; **107** BAL/Giraudon; **108** Joann Fletcher; **109** ÄM/Peter Garbe; **110** BM; **111** RMN/ML/Chuzeville; **113** BM;

115 WFA; **118–9** Archivo Iconográfico SA, Barcelona; **121** ÄM/JL; **123** Axiom, London/James Morris; **124** WFA/ Luxor Museum of Ancient Egyptian Art; **125** R Meldrum, Lanarkshire; **127** AKG/ Luxor Museum of Ancient Eyptian Art/Erich Lessing; **128** RMN/ML; **129** Scala, Florence/EM; **130** Scala, Florence/EM; **132** BM; **134** Egyptian Culture Centre, Waseda University; **135** Egyptian Culture Centre, Waseda University; **137** ET/ML; **138** ÄM; **140–141** AKG/Erich Lessing; **142** BM; **143** Peter Clayton, Hertfordshire; **144** Joann Fletcher/NILE; **145** RMN/ ML/Chuzeville; **146** RMN/ML/ Chuzeville; **147** BAL/ ML/Peter Willi; **149** BAL/BM; **150** BM; **151** AKG; **154** RHPL/FL Kenett; **155** JL/EM; **157** Michael Holford, Essex/ML; **158** EM; **159** BAL/ Giraudon/EM; **160** Peter Clayton, Hertfordshire/EM; **161** Earl of Carnarvon, Highclere Castle, Berkshire; **162** BM; **164–5** BAL/ Giraudon/ML

Every effort has been made to trace the holders of any copyright material included in this book. However, if there are any omissions we will be happy to rectify them in future editions.